MINISTER'S MANUAL

MINISTER'S MANUAL

Compiled and Edited by
WILLIAM E. PICKTHORN

Volume 1
SERVICES FOR SPECIAL OCCASIONS

Volume 2
SERVICES FOR WEDDINGS
AND FUNERALS

Volume 3
SERVICES FOR MINISTERS
AND WORKERS

MINISTER'S MANUAL

Compiled and Edited by
WILLIAM E. PICKTHORN

Volume 3
SERVICES FOR MINISTERS
AND WORKERS

GOSPEL PUBLISHING HOUSE
Springfield, Missouri 65802

02-0549

PREFACE

"It hardly needs to be said that set forms of devotion are uncongenial to those who practice a simple mode of worship and who stress spiritual liberty in prayer and preaching.

"Yet, while recognizing this fact it still remains true that there are special occasions where an appointed order is necessary for a well-conducted service. And if this is so, why be content with forms that are crude or badly prepared? Jesus in the Scripture portion known as the Lord's Prayer instructed the disciples: 'When ye pray, say . . .' The prophet Hosea once said to his countrymen: 'Take with you words, and turn to the Lord, and say to Him . . .' Hosea 14:2.

"There need be no morbid fear of lifeless ritual. As long as the spiritual vitality of the church is maintained the use of necessary forms will never become merely formal."

So wrote Myer Pearlman in the foreword to the first minister's manual produced by the Gospel Publishing House, *The Minister's Service Book*. These words, so true then, are just as true today. Every service must be ordered in some way, but no service need be lifeless and mechanical. The minister, guided by the Spirit, can select ceremonies which he feels contain the touch of the Spirit and which are appropriate to an occasion. Under the leading of the Spirit, he may adapt ceremonies to take into account unique circumstances. Perhaps he may even accept the challenge to write a ceremony of his own! Let this manual be a servant, not a master.

WILLIAM E. PICKTHORN
Christian Center
Palo Alto, California

ACKNOWLEDGMENTS

Credit for suggestions as to what should go into this volume is due to a great many ministers whose names are not in this book. They are men who wrote to say what they would like to see included even though they did not, themselves, submit forms for publication.

Credit for inspiration is due to a great many manuals published over a period of almost 90 years and by many different religious denominations. It is not thought that any of the material in this book has been lifted directly from any other manual. Forms sent by ministers who have contributed to the contents of this book were checked against the available manuals to avoid unintentional infringement of copyright. In instances where there were gaps in the materials received, the editor of this manual made outline notes on procedures detailed in various manuals, and, during a period of more than a year, revised the notes three or more times without reference to original sources so that the materials would become more and more his own. If there are forms in this manual resembling those of any other published book it is through sheer coincidence that they possess such similarity. On the other hand, where materials known to be in copyright have been included—as in the case of some hymns and special statements—permission for their use has been obtained from the copyright owners, and such use is acknowledged at appropriate points in the text.

Deep appreciation and fervent thanks are both extended to those who, through the years, have compiled such manuals. May their inspiration continue to affect others as it has me.

W.E.P.

CONTENTS

MINISTERS

WORKERS

CONTENTS

MINISTERS

Ministers

"How beautiful upon the mountains are the feet of him that bringeth good tidings, that publisheth peace; that bringeth good tidings of good, that publisheth salvation; that saith unto Zion, Thy God reigneth! Thy watchmen shall lift up the voice; with the voice together shall they sing: for they shall see eye to eye, when the Lord shall bring again Zion." (Isa. 52:7, 8)

"Son of man, I have made thee a watchman unto the house of Israel: therefore hear the word at my mouth, and give them warning from me. When I say unto the wicked, Thou shalt surely die; and thou givest him not warning, nor speakest to warn the wicked from his wicked way, to save his life; the same wicked man shall die in his iniquity; but his blood will I require at thine hand. Yet if thou warn the wicked, and he turn not from his wickedness, nor from his wicked way, he shall die in his iniquity; but thou hast delivered thy soul. Again, When a righteous man doth turn from his righteousness, and commit iniquity, and I lay a stumblingblock before him, he shall die: because thou hast not given him warning, he shall die in his sin, and his righteousness which he hath done shall not be remembered; but his blood will I require at thine hand. Nevertheless if thou warn the righteous man, that the righteous sin not, and he doth not sin, he shall surely

3

live, because he is warned; also thou hast delivered thy soul." (Ezek. 3:17-21)

"So thou, O son of man, I have set thee a watchman unto the house of Israel; therefore thou shalt hear the word at my mouth, and warn them from me. When I say unto the wicked, O wicked man, thou shalt surely die; if thou dost not speak to warn the wicked from his way, that wicked man shall die in his iniquity; but his blood will I require at thine hand. Nevertheless, if thou warn the wicked of his way to turn from it; if he do not turn from his way, he shall die in his iniquity; but thou hast delivered thy soul." (Ezek. 33:7-9)

"And Jesus went about all the cities and villages, teaching in their synagogues, and preaching the gospel of the kingdom, and healing every sickness and every disease among the people. But when he saw the multitudes, he was moved with compassion on them, because they fainted, and were scattered abroad, as sheep having no shepherd. Then saith he unto his disciples, The harvest truly is plenteous, but the labourers are few; pray ye therefore the Lord of the harvest, that he will send forth labourers into his harvest." (Matt. 9:35-38)

"And he called unto him the twelve, and began to send them forth by two and two; and gave them power over unclean spirits; and commanded them that they should take nothing for their journey, save a staff only; no scrip, no bread, no money in their purse: but be shod with sandals; and not put on two coats. And he said unto them, In what place soever ye enter into an house, there abide till ye depart from that place." (Mark 6:7-10)

"So when they had dined, Jesus saith to Simon Peter, Simon, son of Jonas, lovest thou me more than these? He saith unto him, Yea, Lord; thou knowest that I love thee. He saith unto him, Feed my lambs. He saith to him again the second time, Simon, son of Jonas, lovest thou me? He saith unto him, Yea, Lord; thou knowest that I love thee. He saith unto him, Feed my sheep. He saith unto him the third time, Simon, son of Jonas, lovest thou me? ... And he said unto him, Lord, thou knowest all things; thou knowest that I love thee. Jesus saith unto him, Feed my sheep." (John 21:15-17)

"Take heed therefore unto yourselves, and to all the flock, over the which the Holy Ghost hath made you overseers, to feed the church of God, which he hath purchased with his own blood. For I know this, that after my departing shall grievous wolves enter in among you, not sparing the flock. Also of your own selves shall men arise, speaking perverse things, to draw away disciples after them. Therefore watch, and remember, that by the space of three years I ceased not to warn every one night and day with tears. And now, brethren, I commend you to God, and to the word of his grace, which is able to build you up, and to give you an inheritance among all them which are sanctified." (Acts 20:28-32)

"How then shall they call on him in whom they have not believed? and how shall they believe in him of whom they have not heard? and how shall they hear without a preacher? and how shall they preach, except they be sent? as it is written, How beautiful are the feet of them that preach the gospel of peace, and bring glad tidings of good things!"

(Rom. 10:14, 15)

"And he gave some, apostles; and some, prophets; and some, evangelists; and some, pastors and teachers; for the perfecting of the saints, for the work of the ministry, for the edifying of the body of Christ: till we all come in the unity of the faith, and of the knowledge of the Son of God, unto a perfect man, unto the measure of the stature of the fulness of Christ: that we henceforth be no more children, tossed to and fro, and carried about with every wind of doctrine, by the sleight of men, and cunning craftiness, whereby they lie in wait to deceive; but speaking the truth in love, may grow up into him in all things, which is the head, even Christ: from whom the whole body fitly joined together and compacted by that which every joint supplieth, according to the effectual working in the measure of every part, maketh increase of the body unto the edifying of itself in love." (Eph. 4:11-16)

"And we beseech you, brethren, to know them which labour among you, and are over you in the Lord, and admonish you; and to esteem them very highly in love for their work's sake. And be at peace among yourselves." (1 Thess. 5:12, 13)

"This is a true saying, If a man desire the office of a bishop, he desireth a good work. A bishop then must be blameless, the husband of one wife, vigilant, sober, of good behaviour, given to hospitality, apt to teach; not given to wine, no striker, not greedy of filthy lucre; but patient, not a brawler, not covetous; one that ruleth well his own house, having his children in subjection with all gravity; (for if a man know not how to rule his own house, how shall he take care of the church of God?) not a novice, lest being lifted up with pride he fall into the condemnation of the devil. Moreover he must have a good report of them which are without; lest he fall into reproach and the snare of the devil." (1 Tim. 3:1-7)

"Let the elders that rule well be counted worthy of double honour, especially they who labour in the word and doctrine." (1 Tim. 5:17)

INSTALLATION OF A PASTOR

PREPARATION FOR THE SERVICE

At the time appointed for the service to begin, the minister who is to be installed may enter the sanctuary preceded by and followed by members of the board or boards.

They may sit in seats reserved for them in the front of the auditorium.

THE CHURCH SERVICE

A previously appointed leader shall take charge of the worship period. A suggested order for this service includes:

CONGREGATIONAL SONG (S)

BIBLE LESSON

PRAYER

MUSIC BY THE CHOIR

OFFERING

CONGREGATIONAL HYMN (OR SOLO)

INTRODUCTION

The leader shall introduce the officer who is to preside over the installation. This officer may be a denominational official, a former pastor of the church, a guest minister selected by the denomination or local church; or he may be a lay representative appointed by the governing board.

CERTIFICATION

The officer in charge of the installation ceremony shall read to the congregation a letter certifying the appointment or election. If the office is by appointment, the letter shall be from the appointing body. If the office is by election, the letter shall be from the governing board of the church, and may give a history of the process of selection.

CHARGE TO THE CONGREGATION

The officer shall ask the candidate to rise, and turning to the congregation, he shall say:

While the Reverend————— (name) has been legally chosen to serve as pastor of————— (name of church and name of city), all of us know that the success of his ministry here will not depend upon the legal appointment, but rather on how faithfully those of us who regularly worship in this church cooperate with Christ's work in this place, support the pastor and pray for him. Therefore in installing the pastor, our first act will be to pray for him that God's blessing may be upon his life and ministry in this place.

PREPARATION FOR PRAYER

The pastor-elect may proceed with the board to the altar of prayer and kneel, surrounded by the board members who shall remain standing. Then the officer shall say:

It is the intent of the————— (name of governing board) of this church to dedicate itself, together with the new pastor at the altar of prayer; and to pray God's richest blessing upon the ministry which shall here begin.

Will all those, therefore, who are concerned about the work of God in this community, and who will say, "God helping me, I will support as best I can, through my prayers and otherwise, the work of our minister so that God's work may grow and prosper in this place"—will you please stand for prayer.

PRAYER

As the pastor-elect continues to kneel, the presiding official, or a minister appointed by him, shall pray.

PLEDGE

A member of the board shall assist the pastor-elect to rise from his knees. A second board member shall escort him to the pulpit. A third shall take a large pulpit Bible from the communion table, carry it to the pulpit and open it to the page on which a covenant has been inscribed.

All of the board members shall then stand close to the pastor-elect, but behind him, at the pulpit.

The pastor-elect shall read the covenant aloud in the hearing of the congregation, and shall sign the covenant with a pen supplied by a board member.

A board member shall then close the Bible and return it to the communion table; and all the board members shall take seats in the congregation.

ASSUMPTION OF OFFICE

The new pastor may make brief comments of appreciation. He may make any necessary announcements. Then he shall announce a hymn.

CONGREGATIONAL SONG

A hymn of praise for God's goodness and care for His people is suitable for this occasion. It may be led by the new minister or by a song leader previously selected.

SERMON

At this point the new pastor may preach his inaugural sermon.

—*J. Calvin Holsinger*

COVENANT FOR
PASTOR'S INSTALLATION

I,————— (full name of minister), believing that the Bible is the inspired Word of God, the infallible rule of faith and conduct, and, without mental reservation, holding to the statement of fundamental truths of this church, do, solemnly covenant, in the presence of these witnesses, that, God being my helper, I will preach the full counsel of God.

I do further affirm that I will endeavor to avoid "doctrines of men" and the preaching of useless and vain customs and controversies.

God helping me, I shall ever seek, as long as I fill this pulpit, to emphasize in sermon, in counseling, in program, the principles upon which this church has been founded, namely:

First, that men of this community may learn to understand God, how wonderful He is, and what He has done for them; and

Secondly, that all who have found Christ as their Lord and Saviour should, by the help of the Holy Spirit, strive to be Christlike in attitude, in word, and in deed;

Thirdly, I will encourage the worshipers to "be filled with the Spirit" and live lives of blessing to the church and community.

As————— (number) pastor of————— (name of church), ————— (denomination), ————— (name of city and state), I freely accept as the purpose of my ministry Christ's words as recorded in Luke 4:18, 19:

"The Spirit of the Lord is upon me, because he hath anointed me to preach the gospel to the poor; he hath sent me to heal the brokenhearted, to preach deliverance to the captives, and recovering of sight to the blind, to set at liberty them that are bruised, to preach the acceptable year of the Lord."

In affirmation of these beliefs I do here subscribe my signature.

In the name of the Father, and of the Son, and of the Holy Spirit,

————— (signature of pastor)

by the grace of God————— (number) pastor of ————— (name of church), ————— (denomination). Amen.

—J. Calvin Holsinger

A CHARGE TO A
NEW MINISTER

The following charge may be read by a denominational official as part of the ceremony of installation.

Forasmuch as our Omniscient God hath, in His divine plan, ordained that you should be a leader among His little flock during————(term of office) if Jesus tarries, I charge you to examine yourself and see whether you are willing to carry this responsibility, remembering that reward for service is not all praise. There will be times when your work may be criticized by some unthinking person, even after you have done your best. You may often feel that you are not as appreciated for your endeavor as you deserve. But, fellow laborer, we must remind ourselves that we serve the Lord Jesus Christ and await His return for our rewarding.

Will you, during your term of office, serve Christ and your church with love and consideration? Will you pray daily for divine blessing upon your efforts? Will you seek to extend the kingdom of God? Will you be true to the doctrines and teachings of ————(name of church), and endeavor to make it grow in apostolic fashion as you have been called hereto?

If, under God, this is your intent and purpose in accepting this high calling, you will please signify same by affirming, "I will," and joining in a prayer of consecration.

PRAYER

If a second denominational leader is present he may be called upon to lead in prayer. The pastor of another church of the community may also be invited to pray.

—*D. Leroy Sanders*

INSTALLATION OF A PASTOR

A CEREMONY INCLUDING
RECOGNITION OF THE WIFE AND CHILDREN

ADDRESS

The officiating minister, the pastor-elect and his wife and family, the church treasurer, official board, and any other persons who are to participate in the installation will be seated in assigned seats.

Then the officiating minister, who may be a presbyter or other denominational officer or a guest minister from a neighboring church, shall address the congregation:

For the welfare, comfort, and help of the needy children of men, God has Himself, by His beloved Son our Lord, ordained and instituted the high office of pastor in His body, the Church. The apostle Paul, in his letter to the Church at Ephesus, recognized this office, saying, "And he gave some, apostles; and some, prophets; and some, evangelists; and some, pastors and teachers; for the perfecting of the saints, for the work of the ministry, for the edifying of the body of Christ" (Eph. 4:11, 12).

We have been called together and are here assembled to install in the pastoral office of this church the———— (title: pastor, reverend) ———— (name of minister), our esteemed brother and fellow laborer in the gospel.

CERTIFICATION

First, we must be assured that———— (title)

————— (name) has been regularly chosen to be minister of this church; and therefore ask for certification from the properly delegated officer of this church.

The church secretary shall provide proper certification from the church minutes. He shall stand before the officiating minister and say:

At a special congregational meeting held on ————— (date), the————— (name of church) extended a call to————— (title) ————— (name of minister) to be its pastor for a term of————— (length of term).

The officiating minister shall then say:

The vote of this body is acknowledged as constituting an official call; and we are now ready to proceed with the installation. ————— (title and name), will you now come to receive your charge.

CHARGE

The minister-elect shall step forward, facing the pulpit.

The officiating minister shall then say as follows:

Since we have heard the Word of our Lord concerning the office of the holy ministry, I ask you therefore, dear brother————— (name), in the presence of this congregation:

Are you now ready to take upon you the office of pastor of————— (name of church) and faithfully serve this congregation? Will you preach and teach the pure Word of God in accordance with the tenets of the————— (name of denomination), and adorn the doctrine of our Saviour by a holy life and godly conversation?

The minister-elect shall answer:

Yes, with the help of God, I will.

INSTALLATION

The officiating minister shall continue:

Upon the command and ordinance of God, I now install you in the office of minister and pastor of —————(name of church), charging you to be diligent and faithful in the same, as you shall give account to Christ the righteous judge at His appearing.

And shaking hands with the pastor-elect, the officiating minister shall say:

The blessing of the Lord be upon you, that you may bring forth much fruit and that your fruit may remain.

RECOGNITION OF THE WIFE

The officiating minister shall call the wife of the new minister to her husband's side, saying:

Since God, in His good providence has given you, —————(name of new pastor), a faithful and true helpmeet, we will now request that—————(wife's name) take her place at your side.

After the wife has come to stand by the side of the new pastor, the officiating minister shall continue, saying:

—————(wife's name), the work of the minister is strengthened and supplemented and enlarged by the faithful support and prayer assistance of a true, noble wife. We know that your spiritual character, your consecration, your sharing the burden of the pastorate with your beloved husband will enable him to have the greatest possible ministry to the glory of God.

I now charge you to be true to your trust. Will you minister in any way in which the Lord will give you opportunity? Will you "feed the lambs" as you instruct the young of this congregation? Will you labor among the women in personal work and visitation, as the Lord shall lead?

The wife of the new pastor shall answer:

Yes, with God's grace and help, I will.

The officiating minister shall then shake the wife's hand, saying:

In the Body of Christ there are helps and governments. I pray that the Lord will grant you His anointing for the ministry to which He has called you.

Recognition of the Children

The officiating minister shall call the children of the new minister to stand by their parents, saying:

I now ask————— (names of children), the children of this minister and his wife to join their parents, standing at their side.

————— (names of children), your parents have given their lives to the work of God. Nothing will give them greater joy than to have you follow in their steps. Even now you can help them in their work. Do you love the Lord Jesus with all your hearts?

The children shall answer in unison:

Yes, we do.

The officiating minister shall continue:

Will you obey your parents, and do your best to win other boys and girls to Christ?

The children shall answer in concert:

Yes, we will.

The officiating minister, laying hands upon the children, shall say:

My dear children, I give you the words of the great apostle Paul: "That from a child thou hast known the holy scriptures, which are able to make thee wise unto salvation through faith which is in Christ Jesus" (2 Tim. 3:15) .

CHARGE TO THE BOARD

The officiating minister shall call the board members forward, saying:

I now ask the board members to take their places directly behind the pastor and his family.

After the board members have assembled, the officiating minister shall continue:

I charge you to be considerate of the temporal comfort and support of this man of God. You are exhorted in the Word of God to "obey them that have the rule over you, and submit yourselves: for they watch for your souls, as they that must give account" (Heb. 13:17) .

CHARGE TO THE CONGREGATION

The officiating minister shall ask the congregation to stand. Then he shall address the people as follows:

I commend you to the————— (name) ————— (name of minister) as your chosen pastor, and charge you in the name of the Lord to be ever mindful of what the Word of God demands of you as members of his flock. Be ready and diligent in your hearing of God's Word. Give your pastor your aid and influence in the instruction of the young and in encouragement to the new converts to the faith. Cease not to pray for him, that his ministry among you may be abundantly blessed. Esteem and love him as the undershepherd of your souls.

PRAYER

The new minister and his family may kneel for prayer. Visiting ministers may all be invited to lay hands upon them as the officiating minister, or a person appointed by him, prays.

—*Robert S. Beisel*

RECEPTION AND INSTALLATION
OF AN ASSOCIATE PASTOR

In the inspired history of the Early Church, God used men, human agency. These men came from every walk of life—from the humble fishermen, the hated tax-gatherers, to the high, heady, and educated scholars. These vessels of clay He filled with His Spirit, imbued with His wisdom, imparted of His nature, and charged with His power. In less than one hundred years, this company had turned the world upside down.

So we, who are called into this same ministry of reconciliation, need to see what manner of men we ought to be. Paul writes that we must be brave, not double-tongued, ruling our own houses well, blameless, as undershepherds, realizing that we are answerable to the Chief Shepherd, and that we preach with a "woe is me" in our souls, for we must hold the mystery of faith in a pure conscience.

And I also charge you, dear people of God, unto whose service this brother has entered, that you follow him with your prayers, that you assist him with your cooperation, and that you esteem him highly for his work's sake. And may the blessing of God rest upon us all, as we labor together for the extension of God's kingdom and for the spiritual progress of this assembly.

"Now the God of patience and consolation grant

you to be like-minded one toward another according to Christ Jesus: that ye may with one mind and one mouth glorify God, even the Father of our Lord Jesus Christ" (Rom. 15:5, 6).

—Glenn M. Horst

WORKERS

Church Officers

GENERAL

"Whatsoever thy hand findeth to do, do it with thy might." (Eccl. 9:10)

"After these things the Lord appointed other seventy also, and sent them two and two before his face into every city and place, whither he himself would come. Therefore said he unto them, The harvest truly is great, but the labourers are few: pray ye therefore the Lord of the harvest, that he would send forth labourers into his harvest. Go your ways: behold, I send you forth as lambs among wolves. Carry neither purse, nor scrip, nor shoes: and salute no man by the way. And into whatsoever house ye enter, first say, Peace be to this house. And if the son of peace be there, your peace shall rest upon it: if not, it shall turn to you again. And in the same house remain, eating and drinking such things as they give: for the labourer is worthy of his hire. Go not from house to house. And into whatsoever city ye enter, and they receive you, eat such things as are set before you: and heal the sick that are therein, and say unto them, The kingdom of God is come nigh unto you. And the seventy returned again with joy, saying, Lord, even the devils are subject unto us through thy name. And he said unto them, I beheld Satan as lightning fall from heaven. Behold, I give unto you power to tread on serpents and scorpions, and over all the power of the enemy: and nothing shall by any means hurt you. Notwithstanding in this rejoice not, that the spirits are subject unto you; but rather rejoice, because your names are written in heaven." (Luke 10:1-9, 17-20)

"Having then gifts differing according to the grace that is given to us, whether prophecy, let us prophesy according to the proportion of faith; or ministry, let us wait on our ministering: or he that teacheth, on teaching; or he that exhorteth, on exhortation: he that ruleth, with diligence; he that sheweth mercy, with cheerfulness. Let love be without dissimulation. Abhor that which is evil; cleave to that which is good. Be kindly affectioned one to another with brotherly love; in honour preferring one another; not slothful in business; fervent in spirit; serving the Lord; rejoicing in hope; patient in tribulation; continuing instant in prayer; distributing to the necessity of saints; given to hospitality. Bless them which persecute you: bless, and curse not. Rejoice with them that do rejoice, and weep with them that weep. Be of the same mind one toward another. Mind not high things, but condescend to men of low estate. Be not wise in your own conceits. Recompense to no man evil for evil. Provide things honest in the sight of all men. If it be possible, as much as lieth in you, live peaceably with all men."

(Rom. 12:6-18)

"And God hath set some in the church, first apostles, secondarily prophets, thirdly teachers, after that miracles, then gifts of healings, helps, govern-ments, diversities of tongues. Are all apostles? are all prophets? are all teachers? are all workers of miracles? have all the gifts of healing? do all speak with tongues? do all interpret? But covet earnestly the best gifts." (1 Cor. 12:28-31)

"As every man hath received the gift, even so minister the same one to another, as good stewards of the manifold grace of God. If any man speak, let him speak as the oracles of God; if any man minister, let him do it as of the ability which God giveth: that God in all things may be glorified through Jesus Christ, to whom be praise and dominion for ever and ever. Amen." (1 Peter 4:10, 11)

DEACONS

"And in those days, when the number of the disciples was multiplied, there arose a murmuring of the Grecians against the Hebrews, because their widows were neglected in the daily ministration. Then the twelve called the multitude of the disciples unto them, and said, It is not reason that we should leave the word of God, and serve tables. Wherefore, brethren, look ye out among you seven men of honest report, full of the Holy Ghost and wisdom, whom we may appoint over this business. But we will give ourselves continually to prayer, and to the ministry of the word. And the saying pleased the whole multitude: and they chose Stephen, a man full of faith and of the Holy Ghost, and Philip, and Pro-chorus, and Nicanor, and Timon, and Parmenas, and Nicolas a proselyte of Antioch; whom they set before the apostles: and when they had prayed, they laid their hands on them. And the word of God increased; and the number of the disciples multiplied in Jerusalem greatly; and a great company of the priests were obedient to the faith."

(Acts 6:1-7)

"Likewise must the deacons be grave, not double-tongued, not given to much wine, not greedy of filthy lucre; holding the mystery of the faith in a pure conscience. And let these also first be proved; then let them use the office of a deacon, being found blameless. Even so must their wives be grave, not slanderers, sober, faithful in all things. Let the deacons be the husbands of one wife, ruling their children and their own houses well. For they that have used the office of a deacon well purchase to themselves a good degree, and great boldness in the faith which is in Christ Jesus."   (1 Tim. 3:8-13)

INSTALLATION OF OFFICERS

DECLARATION

The purpose of this meeting is to recognize the call of God, received and accepted, by members of this church to places of leadership as officers of the church.

The call was given by nominations made after earnest prayer for guidance from the Lord; and by the confirming vote of this congregation.

The offices to which these people have been chosen are those which are essential to the proper functioning of the body. They are *(the list of offices and the names of people selected to fill them shall here be read)* .

These persons have been called, not merely as servants of this congregation, but as servants of the Lord Jesus Christ. They stand ready to pledge their most earnest efforts to carry out the duties entrusted to them. Let us in turn pledge our support of each of them in his particular ministry, and pray God's blessing upon each of their lives.

PRAYER

Prayer should be for God's special guidance. It may be for all of the officers as a group, or it may be for each of them individually.

STATEMENT OF DUTIES

The officers shall be addressed as follows:
It is your duty always to remember that your

first responsibility is to God. You must walk under the anointing and direction of the Holy Spirit. You must be willing to stand alone if need be; but you must never be an authority unto yourself. You who are leaders must work with others. You must check your leadings of the Spirit by conferences with others and be guided by their counsel.

All of you must be one in purpose, maintaining unity of spirit even though there may at times arise differences in understanding.

You must at all times be ready to counsel with the minister, and follow his directions as the ruling elder of the local congregation.

As the consequence of your obedience to the call of God and your walk in the Holy Spirit, it is expected that you will be always concerned for the spiritual welfare of the church; that you will foster the principle of stewardship of time, talents, and of moneys; and that you will be an example as a loyal and devoted follower of the Lord.

CHARGE TO THE OFFICERS

A denominational officer or some other speaker appointed for the purpose shall now address the officers, saying:

Having prayerfully considered the nature and purpose of the work for which you have been chosen, will you consider your election (appointment) a call from God? Will you accept the responsibilities of your particular position as responsibilities given to you by God? Will you seek to do the work of your ministry in the power of the Holy Spirit, and as unto the Lord Jesus Christ? If you will accept this charge, please answer, "I do."

Each of the officers shall respond by answering, either in unison or one at a time, as directed by the leader:

I do.

CHARGE TO THE CONGREGATION

Another denominational officer may come forward to give a charge to the congregation, which shall be instructed to stand as he says to the people:

A body which calls from among its members those to whom it gives special ministries must support the people who have been chosen. Will you recognize these people as especially chosen to be ————— (names of the various offices)? Will you rejoice in the fact that they will be used by God? Will you encourage them in the exercise of their duties? Will you support them by your prayers? Will you assist them in the ministries to which they may call you as helpers? Please affirm this support by answering together, "We will."

Members of the congregation shall answer in unison, saying:

We will.

CONCLUDING ADDRESS

The officer in charge of the installation service shall address both the officers and the congregation, saying:

May God grant to each one of you who is an officer and to every member of this congregation power to carry out the trust which you undertake in the name of His Son Jesus. May He grant you understanding, wisdom, and a special dispensation of His divine love in all that you do.

PRAYER

The service should conclude with prayer for the entire body that it should function under its divine Head in such a way that every member will do the work required of it by God. The prayer should end with thanksgiving for the assurance that God will inspire and guide.

—William E. Pickthorn

Church School Staff

BIBLE REFERENCES

"Go ye therefore, and teach all nations, baptizing them in the name of the Father, and of the Son, and of the Holy Ghost: teaching them to observe all things whatsoever I have commanded you: and, lo, I am with you alway, even unto the end of the world. Amen." (Matt. 28:19, 20)

"Having then gifts differing according to the grace that is given to us, whether prophecy, let us prophesy according to the proportion of faith; or ministry, let us wait on our ministering: or he that teacheth, on teaching; or he that exhorteth, on exhortation: he that giveth, let him do it with simplicity; he that ruleth, with diligence; he that sheweth mercy, with cheerfulness." (Rom. 12:6-8)

"And God hath set some in the church, first apostles, secondarily prophets, thirdly teachers, after that miracles, then gifts of healings, helps, governments, diversities of tongues." (1 Cor. 12:28)

"Let the word of Christ dwell in you richly in all wisdom; teaching and admonishing one another in psalms and hymns and spiritual songs, singing with grace in your hearts to the Lord. And whatsoever ye do in word or deed, do all in the name of the Lord Jesus, giving thanks to God and the Father by him." (Col. 3:16, 17)

"Take heed to the ministry which thou hast received in the Lord, that thou fulfil it."   (Col. 4:17)

"These things command and teach." (1 Tim. 4:11)

"These things teach and exhort."   (1 Tim. 6:2)

"And the things that thou hast heard of me among many witnesses, the same commit thou to faithful men, who shall be able to teach others also."

(2 Tim. 2:2)

INSTALLATION OF OFFICERS

VOLUNTARY

PROCESSIONAL

Members of the Sunday school staff shall enter the sanctuary and march, either single file or two abreast, to reserved seats at the front of the sanctuary. The staff may be preceded by the pastor and/or the church board. If there is a council of Christian education or an education committee it should participate in the processional.

DOXOLOGY

The minister, or a person appointed by him, shall ask the congregation to stand for the singing of the doxology. Then the congregation should be asked to remain standing for prayer.

INVOCATION

This should be a brief prayer of two or three sentences. It may honor God as the great Teacher of men, and ask that the hearts of those present be open to His teaching, through His Son, Jesus Christ, our Lord.

HYMN

"I Love to Tell the Story," or "Wonderful Words of Life," or some other hymn on the Word of God is suggested.

RESPONSIVE READING

The responsive reading should be printed in a worship folder and given to the congregation so that all may join in the reading.

PASTOR: "I beseech you therefore, brethren, by the mercies of God, that ye present your bodies a living sacrifice, holy, acceptable unto God, which is your reasonable service." (Rom. 12:1)

PEOPLE: "And be not conformed to this world: but be ye transformed by the renewing of your mind, that ye may prove what is that good, and acceptable, and perfect, will of God." (Rom. 12:2)

PASTOR: "Search the scriptures; for in them ye think ye have eternal life: and they are they which testify of me." (John 5:39)

PEOPLE: "Study to shew thyself approved unto God, a workman that needeth not to be ashamed, rightly dividing the word of truth." (2 Tim. 2:15)

PASTOR: "Let the word of Christ dwell in you richly in all wisdom; teaching and admonishing one another in psalms and hymns and spiritual songs, singing with grace in your hearts to the Lord." (Col. 3:16)

PEOPLE: "As every man hath received the gift, even so minister the same one to another, as good stewards of the manifold grace of God. If any man speak, let him speak as the oracles of God; if any man minister, let him do it as of the ability which God giveth: that God in all things may be glorified through Jesus Christ, to whom be praise and dominion for ever and ever." (1 Peter 4:10, 11)

PASTOR: "I charge thee therefore before God, and the

Lord Jesus Christ, who shall judge the quick and the dead at his appearing and his kingdom; preach the word; be instant in season, out of season; reprove, rebuke, exhort with all longsuffering and doctrine." (2 Tim. 4:1, 2)

PEOPLE: "Having then gifts differing according to the grace that is given to us, whether prophecy, let us prophesy according to the proportion of faith; or ministry, let us wait on our ministering: or he that teacheth, on teaching." (Rom. 12:6, 7)

PASTORAL PRAYER

This prayer should be for the world in its need of Christ and His gospel; for the community in which the church is located. It should include the needs of the congregation. And it might conclude with the Lord's Prayer.

ANTHEM

OFFERING

HYMN

PRESENTATION OF THE STAFF

One of the officers of the church may be appointed to read the names of the staff. Each person may rise as his or her name is read, and remain standing until all the names have been read, when all may be seated.

SERMON

The sermon may be on "The Church as God's School," "Teaching in the Great Commission," "Workers Together with God," etc.

READING OF WORKERS' COVENANT

NOTE: *A sample covenant for Sunday school teachers will be found at the end of this section of the manual.*

Copies of the covenant may be placed in the hands of the staff; or it may be printed in the church bulletin so that all may see. it. Reading may be done by a board member, or chairman of the Christian Education Committee, or by members of the staff reading assigned portions in turn.

RESPONSE

At the conclusion of the reading of the covenant the staff, led by the superintendent or some other executive officer, shall stand and read in unison the following response:

STAFF: Trusting God for strength, we, as teachers and officers of the church school of————— (name of church) , will, to the best of our ability, endeavor to be true to God, loyal to our church, and faithful to our duties. Thus we accept this covenant as our contract and guide.

COMMISSION

The members of the staff shall remain standing as the pastor, or a person delegated by him, speaks as follows:

In the name of————— (name of the church) and of its church school, I commend you to the duties and labors pertaining to your office in the assurance that, as you perform the ministries which you have accepted, God's richest blessings will attend your every way.

PRAYER OF CONSECRATION

This prayer should be one of thanksgiving for those who have accepted a call to service, a request that they may be empowered by the Holy Spirit, and an invoking of God's blessing upon each of them.

BENEDICTION

—William E. Pickthorn

SUNDAY SCHOOL STAFF DEDICATION

ADDRESS

The pastor shall tell the purpose of this service, indicating that it is to set apart to their ministries people who have previously indicated their willingness to become laborers in the Lord's harvest. The minister may read, or have someone else read, the names of the persons who come for dedication.

CHARGE TO THE STAFF

The minister shall say:

The Lord who called the twelve, who commissioned and sent forth the seventy, who empowered the one hundred and twenty for special service and who by the Holy Spirit selected the leaders of the Apostolic Church, continues to call men and women into His service today. On occasion He speaks through a still small voice, and then the personal call is confirmed by the elders of the church. At times the call is through appointment by the church. At times the call is by election. Yet it is the call of God made apparent by the action of men.

As great a task as any church can offer is the task of ministering to its members through the Sunday school; and its very importance demands that it be accepted as a call from God. Its service must be service unto the Lord. And it must be undertaken only in the power of the Holy Spirit.

Will you who have been chosen to minister in

this Sunday school so accept this call? If so, please stand and indicate your willingness to do so.

STAFF RESPONSE

The staff members shall stand and read aloud in unison as follows:

I accept the call to serve this church through its Sunday school as a call from God to His service; and in humble dependence on Him I pledge myself to the ministry to which I have been called.

CHARGE TO CHURCH BOARD

The staff members shall remain standing, and the church board members shall be asked to come to stand with the staff. Then the minister shall say:

The Sunday school is one of the ministries of this church over which you have supervision. For this reason you have a solemn responsibility to back each one of these people in prayer and to make every possible provision for the effectiveness of his work, remembering that the teaching ministry is the principal means by which "we all come in the unity of faith, and of the knowledge of the Son of God, unto a perfect man, unto the measure of the stature of the fulness of Christ" (Eph. 4:13).

Will you please indicate to these teachers and officers and to the members of this congregation your willingness to so do.

Led by a member who has been selected in advance, the members of the board shall say:

I pledge myself to pray for the Sunday school and its staff, and to join with the other members of this board in making every possible provision for the success of the teaching ministry in this church.

CHARGE TO THE CONGREGATION

To the congregation the minister shall say:

Sunday school is the church studying. Thus Sunday school is not only a department of the church but also an activity, and one in which every member of the body has a part. For this cause every member has a responsibility to pray for the Sunday school, attend its classes, support its ministry, and assist its teachers and officers in their labors for us all. Those who accept this responsibility are invited to stand and thus join the pastor, the board members, and the Sunday school staff as we pledge ourselves to God and to each other to the work of this school and are set apart in prayer to our respective ministries.

PRAYER

This prayer should be one of dedication of the teachers and officers, setting them apart to ministry for the Lord.

—William E. Pickthorn

DEDICATION OF
OFFICERS AND TEACHERS

MINISTER: "The law of the Lord is perfect, converting the soul: the testimony of the Lord is sure, making wise the simple." (Ps. 19:7)

TEACHERS: "The statutes of the Lord are right, rejoicing the heart: the commandment of the Lord is pure, enlightening the eyes." (Ps. 19:8)

MINISTER: "And thou shalt teach them diligently unto thy children, and shalt talk of them when thou sittest in thine house, and when thou walkest by the way, and when thou liest down, and when thou risest up." (Deut. 6:7)

TEACHERS: "Let the words of my mouth, and the meditation of my heart, be acceptable in thy sight, O Lord, my strength, and my redeemer."
(Ps. 19:14)

MINISTER: Officers and teachers of the Sunday school, you have been chosen by this church to be the chief workers of the church for the religious instruction of the children and young people of our number. This is a solemn responsibility. You have been asked to undertake it because you have been thought to be, of all the men and women of the church, those best able to discharge it. Do you accept this charge?

TEACHERS: We do, and by God's help we will labor diligently to be worthy of this trust and faithfully do this work.

MINISTER: Will you undertake to be loyal and zealous servants of the church and of our Lord in doing this work? Will you be regular in attendance, diligent in preparation? Will you labor so to conduct yourself before those who wait upon you for their religious leadership that they may come to know you as a friend and counselor and may be led to a fuller knowledge of God's Word and a better understanding of His way of life?

TEACHERS: All this we promise and with God's help we will earnestly endeavor to do His will.

MINISTER: In the name of the church, then, I hereby dedicate you to serve as officers and teachers of the Sunday school of————— (name of church and city). You have been called to a great responsibility. You have also been called to a happy privilege. You are to be teachers and friends of our young people. They will remember you in love and gratitude throughout their lives. The church is grateful for your devotion. You will rejoice in doing God's work. May His Spirit guide you and His richest blessings be upon you, now and as you continue your ministry.

—Church Management[1]

---

[1] *Church Management*, July, 1947, p. 88. Used by permission.

SUNDAY SCHOOL TEACHER'S COVENANT

As a Sunday school teacher, I humbly and earnestly pledge myself to the following standard which our Sunday school has adopted:

1. I will carefully prepare my lesson and make each class session a matter of earnest prayer.
2. I will manifest a concern for the spiritual welfare of the members of my class, seeking to bring about the salvation of each pupil who does not know Christ and to encourage the Christian growth of those who do.
3. I will teach in accordance with the doctrines of my church and will be an example in conversation, Christian deportment, and prayer.
4. I will encourage my pupils to be faithful in attendance, punctuality, bringing Bibles, preparing lesson, giving offerings, and staying for morning worship.
5. I will attend our Sunday morning and evening services and use my influence to urge the members of my class to be present. I will support the midweek services of my church.
6. I will be personally responsible (or cooperate in a group plan) for the weekly contact of absentees and visitors in my class and for visitation in the home of each pupil at least once every six months.
7. I will be faithful in attending the monthly workers conferences and workers training classes offered by my school.

8. If through sickness or other emergency I am unable to teach my class, I will notify my superintendent as soon as possible.

9. If for any reason I can not fulfill my duties, I will confer with my superintendent and will surrender my class should that seem advisable.

10. I will faithfully fulfill my duties as teacher for the period of my appointment which automatically terminates September 30. If it is impossible for me to accept reappointment, I will notify the superintendent one month in advance.

_____

(Signed)

Appointed from——————to September 30, 19————

Youth Department Officers

"Wherewithal shall a young man cleanse his way? by taking heed thereto according to thy word."

(Ps. 119:9)

"The glory of young men is their strength."

(Prov. 20:29)

"Rejoice, O young man, in thy youth; and let thy heart cheer thee in the days of thy youth, and walk in the ways of thine heart, and in the sight of thine eyes: but know thou, that for all these things God will bring thee into judgment."

(Eccl. 11:9)

"It is good for a man that he bear the yoke in his youth."

(Lam. 3:27)

"Let no man despise thy youth; but be thou an example of the believers, in word, in conversation, in charity, in spirit, in faith, in purity."

(1 Tim. 4:12)

"Flee also youthful lusts: but follow righteousness, faith, charity, peace, with them that call on the Lord out of a pure heart. But foolish and unlearned questions avoid, knowing that they do gender strifes. And the servant of the Lord must not strive; but be gentle unto all men, apt to teach, patient, in meekness instructing those that oppose themselves; if God peradventure will give them repentance to the acknowledging of the truth; and that they may

51

recover themselves out of the snare of the devil, who are taken captive by him at his will."

(2 Tim. 2:22-26)

"And that from a child thou hast known the holy scriptures, which are able to make thee wise unto salvation through faith which is in Christ Jesus."

(2 Tim. 3:15)

"Young men likewise exhort to be sober minded. In all things shewing thyself a pattern of good works: in doctrine shewing uncorruptness, gravity, sincerity."

(Titus 2:6, 7)

"I write unto you, young men, because ye have overcome the wicked one. I write unto you, little children, because ye have known the Father."

(1 John 2:13)

"I have written unto you, young men, because ye are strong, and the word of God abideth in you."

(1 John 2:14)

INSTALLATION OF A YOUTH DIRECTOR

CHARGE

The person to be installed in the office of youth director shall stand at one side of the pulpit while the pastor addresses him, saying:

————— (name), by action of the governing board of elders of this church you have been given the title Youth Director. This position has been established as an office in the church, and carries with it the authority to develop a ministry under the Lord. The term "director" implies guidance—the giving of a sense of direction. Youth is understood to include all ages from childhood through young adult. ————— (name of the church), the name of the church which welcomes you into a place of service, further qualifies and amplifies the nature of the office which you are to hold. Your field of activity will be anything that is Christian. Thus, as youth director, you are charged with responsibility to children, young people, and young adults who are associated with this church, to give them a sense of direction in things that are Christian.

Implicit in the title of the office which you are to hold is the responsibility for establishing positions of leadership under your direction, and the giving of a sense of direction to key people who will, in turn, direct others. Thus you are also charged with a responsibility of supervision.

While you are charged with responsibilities to —————(name of the church), your first and great responsibility is to God. No matter what channels or procedures or activities are employed, your one great work is to bring the young people into contact with Christ who said, "And I, if I be lifted up will draw all men unto me." In the words with which the apostle Paul gave his memorable charge to Timothy, I charge you as a minister of Christ: "Preach the word; be instant in season, out of season; reprove, rebuke, exhort with all longsuffering and doctrine."

If, as the Lord is your helper, you are willing to accept this charge will you please make it known to this congregation.

RESPONSE

The youth director shall speak briefly to the congregation, acknowledging the responsibilities and telling of plans for his work.

CHARGE TO OFFICERS OF EXISTING YOUTH GROUPS

The youth director having taken his seat, the pastor, or an officer appointed by him, shall ask all officers of youth groups to stand; and he shall say to them:

The same Scriptures which provide officers for leadership in the church of Jesus Christ also instruct the members of the church to "obey them that have the rule over you." This means that, under God, we are under obligation to carry out the instructions of those whom the Lord has given positions of authority. Recognizing that—————(name of youth direc-

tor) is God's choice for Youth Director at————
(name of church), I charge you who are officers of
————— (names of groups) and all the young people
of this church that you follow wholly the leadership
which God has given. If you, by God's help, will
accept this charge, will you each please answer, "I
do."

*Each of the officers of youth groups shall answer,
saying*:

I do.

In Bible days, Paul the apostle was called by
the Holy Spirit to a place of leadership in the
church. Paul, in turn, taught Timothy, his son in the
gospel. And then Paul said to Timothy, "The things
that thou hast heard of me among many witnesses,
the same commit thou to faithful men who shall
be able to teach others also." This establishes a
chain of leadership so that those who are followers of
one leader are also leaders in their God-given spheres
of activity. Through the spiritual gifts of helps and
governments, the Holy Spirit has provided the abil-
ities required for this leadership. Believing that
you have been made officers in the will of God, I
charge you with the responsibility of exercising these
gifts of leadership. If you, by God's help, will accept
the charge will you each answer, "I will."

*Each of the officers of youth groups shall answer,
saying*:

I will.

The Scriptures require of all leaders that they

exercise diligence in the Lord's work. Will you, as the Lord helps you, give adequately of your time and strength so that the work which you are now undertaking will be successful? If so, please answer, "I will."

Each of the officers of youth groups shall answer, saying:

I will.

PRAYER

The pastor shall ask every member of the congregation who is willing to pray for and work with the officers of the youth groups and under the direction of the youth director to stand for a prayer of consecration of themselves and of the leaders.

The prayer shall be for the youth director, the officers of youth groups, the members of those groups, and the church as a whole.

—*William E. Pickthorn*

INSTALLATION OF YOUNG PEOPLE'S OFFICERS

ORDER OF PROCEDURE

The officers may be assembled in a room apart from the one in which the installation is to take place. At this time a few personal words to each of them by the pastor (or other ranking church officer) would be appropriate.

Just before time for the service to begin, an usher may lead the officers to seats reserved for them at the front of the church. They should be seated in a prearranged order.

At the appointed time the officers shall stand together and move to the altar. There they shall remain standing facing the congregation. Appropriate music may be played as the group comes forward.

Each officer shall be introduced in turn by the pastor who shall give the name, a word about the person's work in the church or a personal commendation, and the title of the office which the person holds.

As each name is called, the officer shall step forward to read an appropriate Scripture:

President—1 Tim. 4:12

Vice president—1 Tim. 6:12-14

Secretary-treasurer—1 Tim. 6:1-10

Program chairman and librarian—2 Tim. 2:20-23

Social director—2 Tim. 1:7, 8

Remarks and a charge by the youth director, a district officer, or some other responsible officer of the church should follow.

The pastor should ask the entire congregation to stand and join him in a prayer of dedication.

Appropriate music may be played as the officers return to their seats in the congregation.

NOTE: *Attention to details will help make the service more effective. A prearranged signal which is not visible to the congregation will help the group to stand promptly and in unison. Practice in reading of the verses, and placing of markers in the Bibles, will improve the officers' responses. The person who is to give the charge should be informed sufficiently in advance so that he can make his words meaningful. The pastor will appreciate receiving a list of the names of the officers and their positions. Those who will assist the pastor with remarks, charge, and prayer should already be seated on the platform or should be instructed to come forward with the officers without having to be called from the congregation. The music played while the group comes forward and while it returns to seats in the congregation should be quiet and worshipful.*

—*D. Fred Leader*

Music and Musicians

"Then sang Moses and the children of Israel this song unto the Lord, and spake, saying, I will sing unto the Lord, for he hath triumphed gloriously: the horse and his rider hath he thrown into the sea. And Miriam the prophetess, the sister of Aaron, took a timbrel in her hand; and all the women went out after her with timbrels and with dances. And Miriam answered them, Sing ye to the Lord, for he hath triumphed gloriously: the horse and his rider hath he thrown into the sea."

(Ex. 15:1, 20, 21)

"And David went up, and all Israel, to Baalah, that is, to Kirjath-jearim, which belonged to Judah, to bring up thence the ark of God the Lord, that dwelleth between the cherubims, whose name is called on it. And they carried the ark of God in a new cart out of the house of Abinadab: and Uzza and Ahio drave the cart. And David and all Israel played before God with all their might, and with singing, and with harps, and with psalteries, and with timbrels, and with cymbals, and with trumpets."

(1 Chron. 13:6-8)

"And David was clothed with a robe of fine linen, and all the Levites that bare the ark, and the singers, and Chenaniah the master of the song with the singers: David also had upon him an ephod of linen. Thus all Israel brought up the ark of the covenant of the Lord with shouting, and with sound of the cornet, and with trumpets, and with cymbals, making a noise with psalteries and harps."

(1 Chron. 15:27, 28)

"And it came to pass, when the priests were come out of the holy place: (for all the priests that were present were sanctified, and did not then wait by course: also the Levites which were the singers, all of them of Asaph, of Heman, of Jeduthun, with their sons and their brethren, being arrayed in white linen, having cymbals and psalteries and harps, stood at the east end of the altar, and with them an hundred and twenty priests sounding with trumpets:) it came even to pass, as the trumpeters and singers were as one, to make one sound to be heard in praising and thanking the Lord; and when they lifted up their voice with the trumpets and cymbals and instruments of musick, and praised the Lord, saying, For he is good; for his mercy endureth for ever: that then the house was filled with a cloud, even the house of the Lord; so that the priests could not stand to minister by reason of the cloud: for the glory of the Lord had filled the house of God."

(2 Chron. 5:11-14)

"And at the dedication of the wall of Jerusalem they sought the Levites out of all their places, to bring them to Jerusalem, to keep the dedication with gladness, both with thanksgivings, and with singing, with cymbals, psalteries, and with harps. And the sons of the singers gathered themselves together, both out of the plain country round about Jerusalem, and from the villages of Netophathi; also from the house of Gilgal, and out of the fields of Geba and Azmaveth: for the singers had builded them villages round about Jerusalem." (Neh. 12:27-29)

"Rejoice in the Lord, O ye righteous: for praise is comely for the upright. Praise the Lord with harp: sing unto him with the psaltery and an instrument of ten strings. Sing unto him a new song; play skillfully with a loud noise." (Ps. 33:1-3)

"Make a joyful noise unto the Lord, all ye lands. Serve the Lord with gladness: come before his presence with singing. Know ye that the Lord he is God: it is he that hath made us, and not we ourselves; we are his people, and the sheep of his pasture. Enter into his gates with thanksgiving, and into his courts with praise: be thankful unto him, and bless his name. For the Lord is good; his mercy is everlasting; and his truth endureth to all generations." (Ps. 100)

"I will sing of mercy and judgment: unto thee, O Lord, will I sing." (Ps. 101:1)

"Ye shall have a song, as in the night when a holy solemnity is kept; and gladness of heart, as when one goeth with a pipe to come into the mountain of the Lord, to the mighty One of Israel." (Isa. 30:29)

"What is it then? I will pray with the spirit, and I will pray with the understanding also: I will sing with the spirit, and I will sing with the understanding also." (1 Cor. 14:15)

"Speaking to yourselves in psalms and hymns and spiritual songs, singing and making melody in your heart to the Lord." (Eph. 5:19)

"Is any among you afflicted? let him pray. Is any merry? let him sing psalms." (James 5:13)

CHOIR DEDICATION

In the Book of Isaiah God said, "Behold, my servants shall sing for joy of heart." In the Book of Proverbs God said again, "The righteous doth sing and rejoice."

In the Book of First Chronicles, He commanded, "Give thanks unto the Lord, call upon his name, make known his deeds among the people. Sing unto him. Sing psalms unto him." In the Book of Psalms He commanded us to come before His presence with singing. The first verse of the eighty-first Psalm further commands, "Sing aloud unto God our strength."

We follow the precedents established by ancient choirs who were regularly employed for the singing in the temple. First Chronicles 9:33 tells us, "And these are the singers, chief of the fathers of the Levites, who remaining in the chambers were free: for they were employed in that work day and night."

Furthermore, these singers were assisted by an orchestra. Read First Chronicles 15:16: "And David spake to the chief of the Levites to appoint their brethren to be the singers with instruments of musick, psalteries and harps and cymbals, sounding, by lifting up the voice with joy."

There is also scriptural basis for our custom of robing our choirs. We read in First Chronicles 15:27: "And David was clothed with a robe of fine linen, and all the Levites that bare the ark, and the singers, and Chenaniah the master of the song with the singers."

God was pleased to have a great chorus choir practice and be engaged in singing the songs of the Lord.

God gave to Heman fourteen sons and three daughters. "All these were under the hands of their father for singing in the house of the Lord, with cymbals, psalteries, and harps, for the service of the house of God, according to the king's order to Asaph, Jeduthun, and Heman. So the number of them, with their brethren that were instructed in the songs of the Lord, even all that were cunning, was two hundred fourscore and eight."

Furthermore, God who was the original psychologist knew that therapy and encouragement are found in song. So the singers went with the army; and not only went with the men of battle, but preceded them. Listen to Second Chronicles 20:21: "And when he had consulted with the people, he appointed singers unto the Lord, and that should praise the beauty of holiness, as they went out before the army, and to say, Praise the Lord; for his mercy endureth for ever."

So it is entirely fitting that we should include in our worship the singing of hymns and anthems unto the God whom we serve.

RESPONSE BY THE MINISTER OF MUSIC

This morning we who are privileged to serve in the ministry of music desire to dedicate ourselves anew, this first Sunday of our choir year. We renew our covenant with God and with you, our pastor, and with this congregation to be good stewards of the talent God has given.

ACT OF DEDICATION

PASTOR: The Lord God, who knows our hearts, is pleased when we return to Him that which He has given. Jesus said, "Out of the abundance of the heart, the mouth speaketh." Truth, to be effective, must be sincerely spoken. Songs, to be blessed of God, must be sincerely sung. Believing this, will you open your hearts to the fullness of God?

CHOIR: We will.

MINISTER OF MUSIC: We pledge ourselves to a conduct of life worthy of those who lead in corporate worship.

CHOIR: To this we pledge ourselves.

MINISTER OF MUSIC: To consistent development of the talent God has given,

CHOIR: We pledge ourselves.

MINISTER OF MUSIC: To faithful attendance at practice and public worship,

CHOIR: We dedicate ourselves.

MINISTER OF MUSIC: To help in the maintaining of reverence in the house of God,

CHOIR: We dedicate ourselves.

MINISTER OF MUSIC: To make known through prayer-filled song, our gratitude and love toward God,

CHOIR: We dedicate ourselves.

PASTOR: In the authority vested in me as pastor of the church in which you worship God, I place upon you this responsibility. You who are called to be singers in the house of God fulfill your vows this day, and may God's blessing rest upon your ministry unto us all. Let us pray.

PRAYER BY THE PASTOR

Father in heaven, Thou hast given us so much that is beautiful and lovely. We thank Thee for music and its way of speaking to our hearts. We thank Thee for these singers who give of their time and talent. Most of all we are thankful, Lord, for Thyself and the privilege of serving Thee in any capacity.

Wilt Thou bless the covenant made this day by these singers who love to sing for Thee?

In Jesus' name we pray. Amen.

—Mark Davidson

CHURCH FUNCTIONS

Ground Breaking

BIBLE REFERENCES

"Where wast thou when I laid the foundations of the earth? declare, if thou hast understanding. Who hath laid the measures thereof, if thou knowest? or who hath stretched the line upon it? Whereupon are the foundations thereof fastened? or who laid the corner stone thereof; when the morning stars sang together, and all the sons of God shouted for joy?"   (Job 38:4-7)

"I will sing of the mercies of the Lord for ever: with my mouth will I make known thy faithfulness to all generations. For I have said, Mercy shall be built up for ever: thy faithfulness shalt thou establish in the very heavens. And the heavens shall praise thy wonders, O Lord: thy faithfulness also in the congregation of the saints. For who in the heaven can be compared unto the Lord? who among the sons of the mighty can be likened unto the Lord? God is greatly to be feared in the assembly of the saints, and to be had in reverence of all them that are about him. O Lord God of hosts, who is a strong Lord like unto thee? or to thy faithfulness round about thee? Thou rulest the raging of the sea: when the waves thereof arise, thou stillest them. Thou hast broken Rahab in pieces, as one that is slain; thou hast scattered thine enemies with thy strong arm. The heavens are thine, the earth also is thine: as for the world and the fulness thereof, thou hast founded them. The north and the south thou hast created them: Tabor and Hermon shall rejoice in thy name." (Ps. 89:1, 2, 5-12)

"Of old hast thou laid the foundation of the earth: and the heavens are the work of thy hands. They shall perish, but thou shalt endure: yea, all of them shall wax old like a garment; as a vesture shalt thou change them, and they shall be changed: but thou art the same, and thy years shall have no end. The children of thy servants shall continue, and their seed shall be established before thee."

(Ps. 102:25-28)

"Who laid the foundations of the earth, that it should not be removed for ever." (Ps. 104:5)

"Praise ye the Lord. Praise ye the Lord from the heavens: praise him in the heights. Praise ye him, all his angels: praise ye him, all his hosts. Praise ye him, sun and moon: praise him, all ye stars of light. Praise him, ye heavens of heavens, and ye waters that be above the heavens. Let them praise the name of the Lord: for he commanded, and they were created. He hath also stablished them for ever and ever: he hath made a decree which shall not pass. Praise the Lord from the earth, ye dragons, and all deeps: fire, and hail; snow, and vapours; stormy wind fulfilling his word: mountains, and all hills; fruitful trees, and all cedars: beasts, and all cattle; creeping things, and flying fowl: kings of the earth, and all people; princes, and all judges of the earth: both young men, and maidens; old men, and children: let them praise the name of the Lord: for his name alone is excellent; his glory is above the earth and heaven. He also exalteth the horn of his people, the praise of all his saints; even of the children of Israel, a people near unto him. Praise ye the Lord." (Ps. 148)

"Whosoever cometh to me, and heareth my sayings, and doeth them, I will shew you to whom he is like: he is like a man which built an house, and digged deep, and laid the foundation on a rock: and when the flood arose, the stream beat vehemently upon that house, and could not shake it: for it was founded upon a rock. But he that heareth, and doeth not, is like a man that without a foundation built an house upon the earth; against which the stream did beat vehemently, and immediately it fell; and the ruin of that house was great."
(Luke 6:47-49)

"For the earth is the Lord's, and the fulness thereof." (1 Cor. 10:26)

"And, Thou, Lord, in the beginning hast laid the foundation of the earth; and the heavens are the works of thine hands: they shall perish; but thou remainest; and they all shall wax old as doth a garment; and as a vesture shalt thou fold them up, and they shall be changed: but thou art the same, and thy years shall not fail." (Heb. 1:10-12)

BREAKING OF GROUND

Invocation

Bible Lesson

"Wherefore David blessed the Lord before all the congregation: and David said, Blessed be thou, Lord God of Israel our father, for ever and ever. Thine, O Lord, is the greatness, and the power, and the glory, and the victory, and the majesty: for all that is in the heaven and in the earth is thine; thine is the kingdom, O Lord, and thou art exalted as head above all. Both riches and honour come of thee, and thou reignest over all; and in thine hand is power and might; and in thine hand it is to make great, and to give strength unto all. Now therefore, our God, we thank thee, and praise thy glorious name. But who am I, and what is my people, that we should be able to offer so willingly after this sort? for all things come of thee, and of thine own have we given thee. For we are strangers before thee, and sojourners, as were all our fathers: our days on the earth are as a shadow, and there is none abiding. O Lord our God, all this store that we have prepared to build thee an house for thine holy name cometh of thine hand, and is all thine own. I know also, my God, that thou triest the heart, and hast pleasure in uprightness. As for me, in the uprightness of mine heart I have willingly offered all these things: and now have I seen with joy thy people, which are present here, to offer willingly unto thee. O Lord God of Abraham, Isaac, and of

Israel, our fathers, keep this for ever in the imagination of the thoughts of the heart of thy people, and prepare their heart unto thee." (1 Chron. 29:10-18)

DOXOLOGY

DECLARATION

MINISTER: To the glory of God the Father, omnipotent, omniscient, and eternal;

To the praise of His only Son, the author and finisher of our faith;

To the fellowship of the Holy Spirit our Comforter, teacher, and guide:

PEOPLE: We dedicate and break this ground.

BREAKING OF GROUND

A person or persons designated in advance shall turn over a shovelful of earth, using shovels which have been provided for them. Then those who have broken ground shall return to stand with the congregation for the completion of the ceremony.

CONSECRATION

Minister and people shall say together:

We the people of this congregation do now, in the presence of God and in reverence to His holy name, dedicate ourselves to the end:

That the house designated for this place shall be a monument to His grace;

That whatever is within our power to further its construction, both by gifts and by service, we will do;

That the church which shall meet in the house shall minister in the power of the Holy Spirit;

That it shall exalt the Lord Jesus Christ, both in its service to God and to man.

HYMN

"All People That on Earth Do Dwell" is suggested as a suitable hymn.

BENEDICTION

—William E. Pickthorn

GROUND BREAKING CEREMONY

HYMN

The entire congregation shall join in the singing of the hymn, "The Church's One Foundation."

BIBLE READING

"For we are labourers together with God: ye are God's husbandry, ye are God's building. According to the grace of God which is given unto me, as a wise masterbuilder, I have laid the foundation, and another buildeth thereon. But let every man take heed how he buildeth thereupon. For other foundation can no may lay than that is laid, which is Jesus Christ. Now if any man build upon this foundation gold, silver, precious stones, wood, hay, stubble; every man's work shall be made manifest: for the day shall declare it, because it shall be revealed by fire; and the fire shall try every man's work of what sort it is. If any man's work abide which he hath built thereupon, he shall receive a reward. If any man's work shall be burned, he shall suffer loss: but he himself shall be saved; yet so as by fire. Know ye not that ye are the temple of God, and that the Spirit of God dwelleth in you? If any man defile the temple of God, him shall God destroy; for the temple of God is holy, which temple ye are."

(1 Cor. 3:9-17)

"Now therefore ye are no more strangers and foreigners, but fellowcitizens with the saints, and of the household of God; and are built upon the foundation of the apostles and prophets, Jesus Christ himself being the chief corner stone; in whom all the building fitly framed together groweth unto an holy temple in the Lord; in whom ye also are builded together for an habitation of God through the Spirit." (Eph. 2:19-22)

History of the Church

A brief history of the church shall be prepared and read by the church historian, or if there is no historian, by a charter member of the church.

Construction Plans

The general contractor or superintendent of construction, or both of them, shall describe the plan of procedure for the erection of the building.

Financing Plan

The church treasurer shall explain the plan by which the construction will be financed.

Words of Greeting

The District Superintendent or other denominational official shall bring greetings. Others may also speak if deemed desirable.

Prayer of Dedication

A denominational official or visiting minister shall be asked to pray the dedicatory prayer.

Bible Reading

"The Lord is my light and my salvation; whom shall I fear? the Lord is the strength of my life; of whom shall I be afraid?" (Ps. 27:1)

"Therefore whosoever heareth these sayings of

mine, and doeth them, I will liken him unto a wise man, which built his house upon a rock: and the rain descended, and the floods came, and the winds blew, and beat upon that house; and it fell not: for it was founded upon a rock. And every one that heareth these sayings of mine, and doeth them not, shall be likened unto a foolish man, which built his house upon the sand: and the rain descended, and the floods came, and the winds blew, and beat upon that house; and it fell: and great was the fall of it!

(Matt. 7:24-27)

BREAKING OF GROUND

The District Superintendent, or his representative, shall turn the first shovelful of dirt. After this the members of the official board and the building committee shall each turn a shovelful of dirt, all digging at the same time.

HYMN

The song, "To the Work, To the Work" is suggested as suitable for the congregation to sing at this time.

BENEDICTION

—*Raymond P. Murray*

ORDER OF WORSHIP FOR
GROUND BREAKING

HYMN

"The Church's One Foundation" is suggested for congregational singing. Choir, soloist, or other vocal selection may be used.

CALL TO WORSHIP

At the conclusion of the hymn the minister shall say:

We are assembled at this place to open the ground which shall receive the foundation of the church, which, by the grace of God, we have determined to build. Since we have been taught that all important undertakings should always begin by seeking divine guidance, let us by Scripture and by prayer invoke God's leadership upon us.

RESPONSIVE BIBLE READING

MINISTER: "The earth is the Lord's, and the fulness thereof; the world, and they that dwell therein.

PEOPLE: For he hath founded it upon the seas, and established it upon the floods.

MINISTER: Who shall ascend into the hill of the Lord? or who shall stand in his holy place?

PEOPLE: He that hath clean hands, and a pure heart; who hath not lifted up his soul unto vanity, nor sworn deceitfully.

MINISTER: He shall receive the blessing from the Lord, and righteousness from the God of his salvation.

PEOPLE: This is the generation of them that seek him, that seek thy face, O Jacob.

MINISTER: Lift up your heads, O ye gates; and be ye lift up, ye everlasting doors; and the King of glory shall come in.

PEOPLE: Who is this King of glory? The Lord strong and mighty, the Lord mighty in battle.

MINISTER: Lift up your heads, O ye gates; even lift them up, ye everlasting doors; and the King of glory shall come in.

PEOPLE: Who is this King of glory?

ALL: The Lord of hosts, he is the King of glory."

(Ps. 24)

Prayer

This prayer may be in the form of an invocation.

Declaration

The minister shall say:

To the glory of God and in the presence of this congregation, I now request that ground be broken for the new————— (name of building, name of church, city, state). Upon you as members of this congregation rests the responsibility and privilege to cause a church to rise here which shall be devoted to the honor and worship of almighty God our Father, and the glory of His blessed Son and our Saviour, Jesus Christ.

Presentation of Shovel

The architect, superintendent of construction, chairman of the building committee, or some other suitable person shall present a shovel to the first of the people who will assist in the breaking of the ground.

BREAKING OF GROUND

The following people shall have been prepared to participate in the actual turning of the earth; and shall come forward in the following order: charter member, chairman of building committee, minister of church, visiting dignitaries, representative of each department of the church.

RESPONSIVE PRAYER

MINISTER AND PEOPLE: Almighty and everlasting God, in communion with the saints in all ages, and remembering the heritage that has been given to us, we offer Thee our praise and thanksgiving.

PEOPLE: O Lord, hear our prayer.

MINISTER: Enable us, by Thy grace, to dedicate ourselves this day to the great task which Thou dost lay upon our hearts and consciences.

PEOPLE: In all that we do, be Thou, O Lord, our strength and help.

MINISTER: Reveal to us the beauty of Thy perfect law, the joy of our living Lord, so that with glad hearts we may move forward in paths of high devotion and great achievement.

PEOPLE: Be thou, O Lord, our Guide and help forevermore.   Amen.

DOXOLOGY

To be sung by the entire congregation.

BENEDICTION

—Raymond P. Murray

81

VARIATIONS IN
GROUND BREAKING PROCEDURES

The exact spot where the ground is to be broken should be determined in advance. This area should be roped off.

Some have chosen to outline the shape of a cross with lime (or other white substance) and have those who do the turning of the soil dig within the designated lines. When they finish they will have formed the pattern of the cross in the earth. The outlined cross should be about ten feet long and at least eighteen inches in thickness.

Some have chosen to have the digging done in a garden plot reserved for the planting of flowers or shrubs at a later date.

Digging may be done within the actual foundation area, if this area has been determined in advance.

The hardness of the soil should be tested, and if it is found to be too hard to be turned with a shovel, it should be prepared by wetting it down well in advance of the ceremony.

A special shovel is often used for the digging. This shovel may be gilded. And it may be kept as a memorial of the occasion.

If a number of people are to dig, each may bring his own shovel. If the building is done in a rural area where the members of the church use shovels on their farms, etc., they may be asked to bring shovels that they have actually used in their work.

When children are involved in the ceremony they may use toy shovels.

Frequently, miniature plastic shovels are given to the people who attend as souvenirs of the occasion.

As each person comes forward to turn his or her shoveful of earth, he may be instructed to say:

"On behalf of————(department or church group), I break this ground."

On occasion, other means have been used for the turning of the soil

If the ground is to be leveled a bulldozer may be used to cut a swath through the area.

Dynamite has been used to blast open a spot in the ground.

When it is desired that every member of the congregation participate in the ceremony an old-fashioned hand plow may be used. The minister may guide the plow while the members pull it by means of a rope which has been attached to it.

If deep test borings must be made, the first of these borings may be utilized as ground breaking; and bits of the soil may be preserved in vials as keepsakes by members of the congregation.

The ground breaking ceremony can draw a congregation together in an act of consecration, as the members corporately determine to work together for the completion of the program of building. It is a step of faith, coupled with work.

Cornerstone Laying

BIBLE REFERENCES

"How amiable are thy tabernacles, O Lord of hosts! My soul longeth, yea even fainteth for the courts of the Lord: my heart and my flesh crieth out for the living God. Yea, the sparrow hath found an house, and the swallow a nest for herself, where she may lay her young, even thine altars, O Lord of hosts, my King, and my God. Blessed are they that dwell in thy house: they will be still praising thee. Selah. For a day in thy courts is better than a thousand. I had rather be a doorkeeper in the house of my God, than to dwell in the tents of wickedness. For the Lord God is a sun and shield: the Lord will give grace and glory: no good thing will he withhold from them that walk uprightly. O Lord of hosts, blessed is the man that trusteth in thee."

(Ps. 84:1-4, 10-12)

"The stone which the builders refused is become the head stone of the corner. This is the Lord's doing; it is marvellous in our eyes. This is the day which the Lord hath made; we will rejoice and be glad in it. Save now, I beseech thee, O Lord: O Lord, I beseech thee, send now prosperity. Blessed is he that cometh in the name of the Lord: we have blessed you out of the house of the Lord. God is the Lord, which hath shewed us light: bind the sacrifice with cords, even unto the horns of the altar. Thou art my God, and I will praise thee: thou art my God, I will exalt thee. O give thanks unto the Lord; for he is good: for his mercy endureth for ever."   (Ps. 118:22-29)

"For we are labourers together with God: ye are God's husbandry, ye are God's building. According to the grace of God which is given unto me, as a wise masterbuilder, I have laid the foundation, and another buildeth thereon. But let every man take heed how he buildeth thereupon. For other foundation can no man lay than that is laid, which is Jesus Christ. Now if any man build upon this foundation gold, silver, precious stones, wood, hay, stubble; every man's work shall be made manifest: for the day shall declare it, because it shall be revealed by fire; and the fire shall try every man's work of what sort it is. If any man's work abide which he hath built thereupon, he shall receive a reward. If any man's work shall be burned, he shall suffer loss: but he himself shall be saved; yet so as by fire. Know ye not that ye are the temple of God, and that the Spirit of God dwelleth in you? If any man defile the temple of God, him shall God destroy; for the temple of God is holy, which temple ye are."   (1 Cor. 3:9-17)

"But now in Christ Jesus ye who sometimes were far off are made nigh by the blood of Christ. For he is our peace, who hath made both one, and hath broken down the middle wall of partition between us; having abolished in his flesh the enmity, even

the law of commandments contained in ordinances;
for to make in himself of twain one new man, so
making peace; and that he might reconcile both
unto God in one body by the cross, having slain
the enmity thereby: and came and preached peace
to you which were afar off, and to them that were
nigh. For through him we both have access by one
Spirit unto the Father. Now therefore ye are no
more strangers and foreigners, but fellowcitizens
with the saints, and of the household of God; and
are built upon the foundation of the apostles and
prophets, Jesus Christ himself being the chief corner
stone; in whom all the building fitly framed together groweth unto an holy temple in the Lord:
in whom ye also are builded together for an habitation of God through the Spirit."   (Eph. 2:13-22)

"The Lord is gracious. To whom coming, as
unto a living stone, disallowed indeed of men, but
chosen of God, and precious, ye also, as lively stones,
are built up a spiritual house, an holy priesthood,
to offer up spiritual sacrifices, acceptable to God
by Jesus Christ. Wherefore also it is contained in
the scripture, Behold, I lay in Sion a chief corner
stone, elect, precious: and he that believeth on him
shall not be confounded. Unto you therefore which
believe he is precious: but unto them which be
disobedient, the stone which the builders disallowed,
the same is made the head of the corner, and a stone
of stumbling, and a rock of offence, even to them
which stumble at the word, being disobedient: where-

unto also they were appointed. But ye are a chosen generation, a royal priesthood, an holy nation, a peculiar people; that ye should shew forth the praises of him who hath called you out of darkness into his marvellous light: which in time past were not a people, but are now the people of God: which had not obtained mercy, but now have obtained mercy."

(1 Peter 2:3-10)

DEDICATION OF A CORNERSTONE

MINISTER: To the glory of God the Father; as a pledge of service to Christ our Lord; in the fellowship of the Holy Spirit,

PEOPLE: We lay this cornerstone.

MINISTER: For a building to house a congregation of the church of which Christ is the chief cornerstone,

PEOPLE: We lay this cornerstone.

MINISTER: For a church where Christ shall be exalted as the eternal Son of the living God,

PEOPLE: We lay this cornerstone.

MINISTER: For a church which will proclaim salvation through the shed blood of Christ,

PEOPLE: We lay this cornerstone.

MINISTER: For a church where prayer shall be offered for the healing of those who are sick,

PEOPLE: We lay this cornerstone.

MINISTER: For a church which will teach a life of separation unto God,

PEOPLE: We lay this cornerstone.

MINISTER: For a church whose members will be encouraged to walk in the fullness of the Holy Spirit,

PEOPLE: We lay this cornerstone.

MINISTER: For a church looking for the coming of the blessed Lord "without sin unto salvation,"

PEOPLE: We lay this cornerstone.

PLACING THE STONE

At this point the cornerstone shall be sealed into place.

MINISTER: Churches are not built of wood and stone and glass alone. The people who make up their congregations are the temples of which Christ is "the stone of the corner." "For other foundation can no man lay than that is laid, which is Jesus Christ."

PEOPLE: We lay this cornerstone. In dedication of ourselves to the Lord, and to the sacrifices and service of building, we lay a cornerstone for our new church.

PRAYER

—William E. Pickthorn

CORNERSTONE LAYING

CALL TO WORSHIP

Fanfare and hymn by a trumpet trio.

BIBLE READING

"Great is the Lord, and greatly to be praised in the city of our God, in the mountain of his holiness. Beautiful for situation, the joy of the whole earth, is mount Zion, on the sides of the north, the city of the great King. God is known in her palaces for a refuge. For, lo, the kings were assembled, they passed by together. They saw it, and so they marvelled; they were troubled, and hasted away. Fear took hold upon them there, and pain, as of a woman in travail. Thou breakest the ships of Tarshish with an east wind. As we have heard, so have we seen in the city of the Lord of hosts, in the city of our God: God will establish it for ever. Selah. We have thought of thy lovingkindness, O God, in the midst of thy temple. According to thy name, O God, so is thy praise unto the ends of the earth: thy right hand is full of righteousness. Let mount Zion rejoice, let the daughters of Judah be glad, because of thy judgments. Walk about Zion, and go round about her: tell the towers thereof. Mark ye well her bulwarks, consider her palaces; that ye may tell it to the generation following. For this God is our God for ever and ever: he will be our guide even unto death." (Ps. 48)

"And Jesus came and spake unto them, saying, All power is given unto me in heaven and in earth.

Go ye therefore, and teach all nations, baptizing them in the name of the Father, and of the Son, and of the Holy Ghost: teaching them to observe all things whatsoever I have commanded you: and, lo, I am with you alway, even unto the end of the world." (Matt. 28:18-20)

PRAYER

One of the deacons of the church shall have been selected in advance to lead in prayer.

ANTHEM

"I Will Build My Church" is suggested as an anthem to be sung by the choir.

HISTORY

The secretary or church historian shall here read a paper on the history of the church.

UNVEILING OF CORNERSTONE

The pastor and the contractor shall act together in removing the covering from the cornerstone.

REPORT ON CONTENTS OF VAULT

The pastor shall report to the congregation on the contents of the cornerstone vault.

Suggested as suitable contents of the box are: printed materials concerning the church, its constitution, application for membership, bulletin, etc.; list of church officers; printed sermon by the pastor; denominational publications—The Pentecostal Evangel, C. A. Herald, Global Conquest, etc.; local newspaper containing story about the church; Bible.

DELIVERY OF VAULT TO BUILDER

The pastor shall give the box containing the articles to be sealed into the cornerstone to the builder.

The builder shall respond with a short talk concerning the building and its significance to the community.

PLACING THE STONE

The stone shall be slid into the niche provided for it; and may be sealed into place at a later date.

DOXOLOGY

The doxology shall be sung by the congregation.

BENEDICTION

The benediction shall be pronounced by a church officer.

—Leland R. Keys

LAYING OF A CORNERSTONE

PROCESSIONAL AND HYMN

The choir shall proceed to its designated seats, singing, "Christ Is Made the Sure Foundation" or other suitable hymn.

Leaders who are to participate in the dedication should follow the choir in the processional.

INVOCATION

BIBLE LESSON

The lesson may be read responsively, with ministers and congregation participating. It could be read by a youth verse choir.

Some churches use two Scripture lessons, one from the Old Testament and one from the Epistles. If this is done, the lessons may be separated by the singing of a "praise" response.

CHORAL SELECTION

SERMON

SOLO

DECLARATION

MINISTER: For a building which shall stand as a monument to faith in the only true God: taught by the prophets, revealed in the person of Christ, preached by ministers of His gospel,

PEOPLE: To the glory of God we lay this cornerstone.

MINISTER: For a building where all may come to praise the name of God, to bow prostrate before

Him, to confess their guilt, obtain pardon, and gain strength for life according to His will,

PEOPLE: For a house of worship, we lay this cornerstone.

MINISTER: For a house where all may be instructed; where the Word of God will be proclaimed as "profitable for doctrine, for reproof, for correction, for instruction in righteousness"; where children may be trained in its fundamentals and where the mature may grow by the "meat" of the Word,

PEOPLE: For a place of teaching, we lay this cornerstone.

MINISTER: For a church devoted to the fulfillment of the great commission; from which the gospel shall be taken to the entire world, to be preached to every creature; into which men, born of the Spirit, shall come as disciples,

PEOPLE: For a center of evangelism, we lay this cornerstone.

MINISTER: For a building where the truths of Christianity shall not only be taught, but practiced; for a place of service to God, for a place of ministry to others,

PEOPLE: For a building dedicated to Christian service, we lay this cornerstone and dedicate the memorials which it contains.

PLACING THE STONE

The minister, standing by the stone, may exhibit to the people the box which is to be placed in the

stone. It may contain such articles as a Bible, history of the church, articles of faith, names of pastor and boards, church roster, and any other documents which might be of interest to future generations. The minister, or one of his staff, may read a list of the articles to be deposited in the box. The box shall be placed in the stone. Then, with the aid of the builder, the minister shall lay the stone in its place.

DEDICATION

MINISTER: May the house which shall be built on this foundation abundantly fulfill the purposes which God has designed for this church.

PEOPLE: To the glory of God we dedicate this corner of the foundation on which will be built the house which we will also dedicate to the honor of His name.

SOLO OR DUET

DOXOLOGY

Any suitable chorus of praise may be sung by the congregation.

BENEDICTION

—William E. Pickthorn

Building Dedication

BIBLE REFERENCES

"Then said Solomon, The Lord hath said that he would dwell in the thick darkness. But I have built an house of habitation for thee, and a place for thy dwelling for ever. And he said, Blessed be the Lord God of Israel, who hath with his hands fulfilled that which he spake with his mouth to my father David. O Lord God of Israel, there is no God like thee in the heaven, nor in the earth; which keepest covenant, and shewest mercy unto thy servants, that walk before thee with all their hearts. Now then, O Lord God of Israel, let thy word be verified, which thou hast spoken unto thy servant David. But will God in very deed dwell with men on the earth? behold, heaven and the heaven of heavens cannot contain thee; how much less this house which I have built! Have respect therefore to the prayer of thy servant, and to his supplication, O Lord my God, to hearken unto the cry and the prayer which thy servant prayeth before thee: that thine eyes may be open upon this house day and night, upon the place whereof thou hast said that thou wouldest put thy name there; to hearken unto the prayer which thy servant prayeth toward this place. Then hear thou from the heavens, even from thy dwelling place, their prayer and their supplications, and maintain their cause, and forgive thy people which have sinned against thee. Now, my God, let, I beseech thee, thine eyes be open, and let thine ears be attent unto the prayer that is made in this place. Now therefore arise, O Lord God, into thy resting place, thou, and the ark of thy strength: let thy priests, O Lord God, be clothed with salvation, and let thy saints rejoice in goodness."

(2 Chron. 6:1, 2, 4, 14, 17-20, 39-41)

"We have thought of thy lovingkindness, O God, in the midst of thy temple. According to thy name, O God, so is thy praise unto the ends of the earth: thy right hand is full of righteousness. Let mount Zion rejoice, let the daughters of Judah be glad, because of thy judgments. Walk about Zion, and go round about her: tell the towers thereof. Mark ye well her bulwarks, consider her palaces; that ye may tell it to the generation following. For this God is our God for ever and ever: he will be our guide even unto death." (Ps. 48:9-14)

"How amiable are thy tabernacles, O Lord of hosts! My soul longeth, yea, even fainteth for the courts of the Lord: my heart and my flesh crieth out for the living God. Yea, the sparrow hath found an house, and the swallow a nest for herself, where she may lay her young, even thine altars, O Lord of hosts, my King, and my God. Blessed are they that dwell in thy house: they will be still praising thee. Selah. Blessed is the man whose strength is in thee; in whose heart are the ways of them. Who passing through the valley of Baca make it a well; the rain also filleth the pools. They go from strength to strength, every one of them in Zion appeareth before God. O Lord God of hosts, hear my prayer: give ear, O God of Jacob. Selah. Behold, O God our shield, and look upon the face of thine anointed. For a day in thy courts is better than a thousand. I had rather be a doorkeeper in the house of my God, then to dwell in the tents of wickedness. For the Lord God is a sun and shield: the Lord will give grace and glory: no good thing will he withhold from them that walk uprightly. O Lord of hosts, blessed is the man that trusteth in thee."   (Ps. 84)

"Make a joyful noise unto the Lord, all ye lands. Serve the Lord with gladness: come before his presence with singing. Know ye that the Lord he is God: it is he that hath made us, and not we ourselves; we are his people, and the sheep of his pasture. Enter into his gates with thanksgiving, and into his courts with praise: be thankful unto him, and bless his name. For the Lord is good; his mercy is everlasting; and his truth endureth to all generations."
(Ps. 100)

"I was glad when they said unto me, Let us go into the house of the Lord. Our feet shall stand within thy gates, O Jerusalem. Jerusalem is builded as a city that is compact together: whither the tribes go up, the tribes of the Lord, unto the testimony of Israel, to give thanks unto the name of the Lord. For there are set thrones of judgment, the thrones of the house of David. Pray for the peace of Jerusalem: they shall prosper that love thee. Peace be within thy walls, and prosperity within thy palaces. For my brethren and companions' sakes, I will now say, Peace be within thee. Because of the house of the Lord our God I will seek thy good."   (Ps. 122)

ACT OF DEDICATION

MINISTER: Because we have built a sanctuary for the worship of God and the service of Jesus Christ, I call upon the congregation here assembled to now stand for the act of dedication.

The congregation shall stand, and remain standing for the reading of the act of dedication.

MINISTER: For the preaching of the gospel of salvation to the unsaved; for the preaching and teaching of the Word of God for the edification of the believer; for the nurture and admonition of young people and children in the faith "once delivered unto the saints,"

PEOPLE: We dedicate this house of God.

MINISTER: For the providing of a church home with a warm spiritual and friendly atmosphere, where needy souls may find their every need met in the Lord Jesus Christ,

PEOPLE: We dedicate this house of God.

MINISTER: That we may the better learn the great principles of the sanctity of the home, the sacredness of the marriage vows, and the hallowing of all family life,

PEOPLE: We dedicate this house.

MINISTER: That we may so develop Christian character, exemplifying the teachings of the Word of God in our daily lives, thereby making us acceptable and approved citizens of both the kingdom of God and of the state,

PEOPLE: We dedicate this house of prayer and worship.

MINISTER: To the preaching of the "whole counsel of God" which most certainly includes all those tenets of faith of the Assemblies of God,

PEOPLE: We sincerely dedicate this place of worship.

MINISTER: To the outreach of the church to the uttermost part of the world, through vision, giving, and going,

PEOPLE: We dedicate this house to the missionary cause of world evangelization.

MINISTER: In gratitude to those whose loving service, prayers, and generous giving have made possible the founding, growth, and development of this church and the completion of this sanctuary,

PEOPLE: We dedicate this house of God.

MINISTER: In loving memory of those who have joined the Church Triumphant, but whose "works do follow them,"

PEOPLE: We dedicate this building.

MINISTER: What is the covenant of this standing congregation?

PEOPLE: We covenant together in this act of dedication to offer ourselves anew in an act of personal dedication that God may be glorified, that Jesus Christ may be served, and that the Holy Spirit shall be honored. We covenant together to do justly, to love mercy, and to walk humbly with our God; He being our helper. Amen.

—Leland R. Keys

RITE OF DEDICATION

PASTOR: "Praise ye the Lord. Praise ye the name of the Lord; praise him, O ye servants of the Lord." (Ps. 135:1)

PEOPLE: "Praise ye the Lord. Praise God in his sanctuary: praise him in the firmament of his power." (Ps. 150:1)

PASTOR: "Except the Lord build the house, they labour in vain that build it." (Ps. 127:1)

PEOPLE: "The Lord hath done great things for us; whereof we are glad." (Ps. 126:3)

PASTOR: "O give thanks unto the Lord, for he is good: for his mercy endureth for ever." (Ps. 107:1)

PEOPLE: "For the Lord is a great God, and a great King above all gods." (Ps. 95:3)

PASTOR: Having been guided of the Lord Jesus Christ, in answer to our prayers of faith, and by His enabling grace, wisdom, and power, to erect this house of worship, we now humbly petition Him, recognizing our own unworthiness, that it shall only be used to the glory, honor, and praise of God our Father, the Lord Jesus Christ our Saviour, and the Holy Spirit our Comforter and Guide.

PEOPLE: We dedicate this house of God.

PASTOR: With gratitude to God for those who have labored, and those who have prayed, and the many faithful stewards who have given of their substance that this house of God might be a reality,

PEOPLE: We gratefully dedicate this house of God.

PASTOR: For the preaching and teaching of the Word of God that souls might be saved and that those saved, both young and old, might be built up in the most holy faith,

PEOPLE: We prayerfully dedicate this house of God.

PASTOR: For the comforting of those who mourn, for the strengthening of those who are weak, for the helping of any who are tempted and tried,

PEOPLE: We reverently dedicate this house of God.

PASTOR: For the development of a missionary vision that will send forth laborers into the whitened harvest fields both at home and around the world with the gospel of God's grace in the Lord Jesus Christ,

PEOPLE: We humbly dedicate this house of God.

PASTOR AND PEOPLE: We, the people of this church and congregation now dedicating ourselves anew, earnestly and unitedly pray that the Almighty God may ever manifest His presence in this place and that our constant aim shall be the exalting of the Lord Jesus Christ, the salvation of the lost, and the edification of the saints of the Lord. Amen.

—Wheaton Bible Church, Wheaton, Ill.

THE WORDS OF DEDICATION

MINISTER: Having been prospered by the good hand of the Lord our God, and being ever mindful of our duty as stewards of the talents that He has entrusted to us,

PEOPLE: With joyous and grateful hearts we consecrate this house of our God, who has loved us, and has blessed us, and led us thus far in the completion of our cherished task.

MINISTER: Believing in God our Father, in whom we live and move and have our being, from whom cometh every good and perfect gift,

PEOPLE: We dedicate this house to His worship, and to the preaching of the gospel of Jesus Christ.

MINISTER: Knowing that there is none other name under heaven, given among men, whereby we must be saved,

PEOPLE: We dedicate this church to evangelism; to the bringing of the saving knowledge of our Lord and Master to the unconverted.

MINISTER: In obedience to the command that has been given to us to go into all the world and make disciples of all nations,

PEOPLE: We dedicate this house to the worldwide program of the Christian church, till all the kingdoms of the world become the kingdom of our Lord and His Christ.

MINISTER: Realizing the obligation to bring up our children in the nurture and admonition of the Lord,

PEOPLE: We dedicate this church to the purpose of Christian education, that the boys and girls of this and coming generations may here study God's Word, make confession of Christ, and be led into paths of purity and usefulness.

MINISTER: In accordance with the commandment of Christ that we love our neighbors as ourselves,

PEOPLE: We dedicate this building to the service of Christian fellowship.

MINISTER AND PEOPLE: And unto Thee, our God, we, the people of this church and congregation and all those who are here met with us, do dedicate ourselves anew, beseeching Thee that Thou wilt not leave us nor forsake us; that Thou wilt incline our hearts unto Thee, to walk in Thy truth, and to keep Thy commandments all the days of our lives, through Jesus Christ our Lord. Amen.

—H. Russell Baker

ORDER OF CEREMONY

PRELUDE

THE CUTTING OF THE RIBBON

The oldest charter member, or a person selected by the vote of the congregation, may be selected to cut the ribbon. The ceremony may be worked out by a youth group featuring a processional of the youth of the congregation.

CONGREGATIONAL SONG

"Amazing Grace" is suggested as a suitable song.

INVOCATION

BIBLE READING

"And he came to Nazareth, where he had been brought up: and, as his custom was, he went into the synagogue on the sabbath day, and stood up for to read. And there was delivered unto him the book of the prophet Esaias. And when he had opened the book, he found the place where it was written, The spirit of the Lord is upon me, because he hath anointed me to preach the gospel to the poor; he hath sent me to heal the brokenhearted, to preach deliverance to the captives, and recovering of sight to the blind, to set at liberty them that are bruised, to preach the acceptable year of the Lord. And he closed the book, and he gave it again to the minister, and sat down. And the eyes of all them that were in the synagogue were fastened on him. And he began to say unto them, This day is this scripture fulfilled in your ears." (Luke 4:16-21)

"If I speak with the tongues of men and of angels,

but have not love, I am become sounding brass, or a clanging cymbal. And if I have the gift of prophecy, and know all mysteries and all knowledge; and if I have all faith, so as to remove mountains, but have not love, I am nothing. And if I bestow all my goods to feed the poor, and if I give my body to be burned, but have not love, it profiteth me nothing. Love suffereth long, and is kind; love envieth not; love vaunteth not itself, is not puffed up, doth not behave itself unseemly, seeketh not its own, is not provoked, taketh not account of evil; rejoiceth not in unrighteousness, but rejoiceth with the truth; beareth all things, believeth all things, hopeth all things, endureth all things. Love never faileth: but whether there be prophecies, they shall be done away; whether there be tongues, they shall cease; whether there be knowledge, it shall be done away. For we know in part, and we prophesy in part; but when that which is perfect is come, that which is in part shall be done away. When I was a child, I spake as a child, I felt as a child, I thought as a child: now that I am become a man, I have put away childish things. For now we see in a mirror, darkly; but then face to face: now I know in part; but then shall I know fully even as also I was fully known. But now abideth faith, hope, love, these three; and the greatest of these is love."

(1 Cor. 13, A.S.V.)

VOCAL SOLO

GREETINGS AND RECOGNITIONS

ANTHEM

ADDRESS

UNVEILING OF MEMORIAL PAINTING

ACT OF DEDICATION

MINISTER: It is right and proper that buildings erected for special services in the name of our Lord and Saviour Jesus Christ should be formally and devoutly set apart for their special uses. For such a dedication we are now assembled. And, as the dedication of this building is vain without the solemn consecration of those whose gifts and labors it represents, let us now give ourselves anew to the service of God: our souls, that they may be renewed after the image of Christ; our bodies, that they may be fit temples for the indwelling Holy Spirit; and our labors and business, that they may tend to the glory of His name and the advancement of His kingdom.

MINISTER AND PEOPLE: We dedicate ourselves anew to that service of our fellowmen wherein can best be performed our true service to God, in obedience to the spirit of the Master when He said, "Thou shalt love the Lord thy God with all thy heart, and thy neighbor as thyself."

MINISTER: We dedicate this building to that ministry of administration upon whose ability and fruitfulness depends the wise conduct of its affairs.

PEOPLE: "Who then is that faithful and wise steward, whom his lord shall make ruler over his household? Blessed is that servant, whom his lord when he cometh shall find so doing."

MINISTER: To the glory of God, our Father, from whom cometh every good and perfect gift,

PEOPLE: We dedicate this building.

MINISTER: To the honor of Jesus Christ, His Son, our Lord and Saviour,

PEOPLE: We dedicate this building.

MINISTER: In gratitude for the labors of all who love and serve this fellowship; in loving remembrance of those who have finished their course; for the promotion of righteousness; for the extension of the kingdom of God,

PEOPLE: We dedicate this building.

MINISTER AND PEOPLE: We now, the people of this congregation, compassed about with a great cloud of witnesses, grateful for our heritage, sensible of the sacrifice of our fathers in the faith, confessing that apart from us their work cannot be made perfect, do dedicate this building to the service of Almighty God; through Jesus Christ our Lord. Amen.

MINISTER: In the faith of our Lord Jesus Christ, I dedicate this building in the memory of———— (name of person—if the building is a memorial) in the name of the Father, and of the Son, and of the Holy Ghost. Amen.

PRAYER OF DEDICATION

DOXOLOGY

BENEDICTION

POSTLUDE

—Leonard Palmer

DEDICATION OF A NEW BUILDING

Acceptance of the Building

The congregation, officiating ministers, chairman of the building committee, chairman of the official board, and any other officers to be recognized in the dedication ceremony shall assemble at the outside of the main door of the church.

At the appointed time the minister shall approach the door and knock, saying:

Open in the name of the Lord of Hosts that we may enter and dedicate this house which together we have built to the glory of His name.

The architect and contractor shall open the doors from the inside, and come out to stand before the officiating group.

The architect shall deliver the keys of the church to the contractor, greeting him by name, shaking his hand, and saying:

————— (name), I give you the keys to the house which you and your helpers have so skillfully built.

The contractor, in the same manner, shall give the keys to the chairman of the building committee, saying:

————— (name), these keys represent the fulfillment of the dream for which you and your committee have worked.

The building committee chairman shall, in a similar manner, deliver the keys to the chairman of the official board, saying:

————— (name), our committee delivers to you

the keys of this building erected for————— (name of church) .

The official board chairman shall deliver the keys to the pastor saying:

————— (name of pastor) , as the delegated representative of the congregation which authorized the building of this house for God, I give you the key to each of its doors, that the door may be opened to God and the space to which the keys give access may be consecrated by an act of dedication.

The pastor shall accept the keys, and say:

On behalf of the congregation and officers of this church, I accept these keys as a symbol of the responsibility which is given to us to unlock the storehouse of the riches of God to the people of our community. And, in the light of this responsibility, we shall proceed with the dedication.

BIBLE LESSON

The minister, or ministers, shall enter the church and pause within the inner doors and read aloud in unison:

"Blessed be the Lord, that hath given rest unto his people . . . according to all that he promised: there hath not failed one word of all his good promise, which he promised . . . The Lord our God be with us, as he was with our fathers: let him not leave us, nor forsake us: that he may incline our hearts unto him, to walk in all his ways, and to keep his commandments, and his statutes, and his judgments, which he commanded our fathers."

(1 Kings 8:56-58)

PROCESSIONAL

Following the reading, the processional shall begin. A proposed order follows:

The ministers shall stand on either side of the aisle, inside the inner door, while the choir and instrumentalists enter.

The choir shall enter the inner doors in processional, singing without accompaniment. The first member to enter shall begin to sing. The voice of each member shall be added as he enters the room. The choir shall proceed to the choir seats, remain standing and continue to sing.

Organist and pianist shall follow the choir, and, at an appropriate place, add accompaniment.

The honored guests and ministers shall follow the choir in the processional.

Ushers shall follow the ministers, proceeding to their appointed stations.

The congregation shall follow.

The choir and congregation shall conclude the singing together, and remain standing for prayer.

PRAYER

The subject of the prayer will depend on the nature of the rest of the service. If the act of dedication is to follow immediately, this should be a prayer of dedication. If there is to be a song service and preaching before the act of dedication, this prayer should be an invocation.

ACT OF DEDICATION

PASTOR: From the Holy Scriptures we learn that it is fitting and proper that houses should be erected for the worship of God, and that such houses should be especially set apart and dedicated to uses which glorify His name. Today we are gathered together in the sight of God to dedicate such a building.

The Scriptures say that, when the temple was rebuilt in the days of Ezra, "the children of Israel, the priests, and the Levites, and the rest of the children of the captivity, kept the dedication of this house of God with joy" (Ezra 6:16).

We are grateful for the opportunity which God has given us to build, for our own generation and for generations yet to come, a house which is the house of God. We rejoice that the work of building has been carried to its completion and that the house is now ready for the ministries to which it shall be dedicated. Therefore it is with great joy that,

PEOPLE: We dedicate to Thee, O Lord, this house of God: to the glory of God the Father who hath called us by His grace; to the honor of Jesus Christ, the Son, who loved us and gave Himself for us; to the praise of the Holy Spirit of promise who is our Comforter and guide.

PASTOR: For the worship of God in praise and prayer; for the preaching of the gospel of the Lord Jesus Christ and the observance of the holy ordinances commanded by Him; for ministry in the power of the Holy Spirit,

PEOPLE: We dedicate this house of God.

PASTOR: For the comfort of those who are in sorrow; for the strengthening of those who are weak; for the encouragement of those who are in the throes of trials or temptations,

PEOPLE: We dedicate this house of God.

PASTOR: For the blessing of God upon the marriages which shall be consummated among us; for the sanctification and protection of the family; for guidance in the establishing of Christian homes,

PEOPLE: We dedicate this house of God.

PASTOR: For the teaching of the eternal truths of God's Word; for the shaping of lives to conform to the image of God's Son; for the directing of Christian action to the everyday fulfillment of God's purposes in man,

PEOPLE: We dedicate this house of God.

PASTOR: For the salvation of the lost who shall come to this house; for the winning of those to whom we will take a personal witness; for the conversion of the heathen by means of the missionary program to which we shall give our support,

PEOPLE: We dedicate this house of God.

PASTOR: In loving memory of all who, with heart and hand, have served this church; with deep gratitude to those whose gifts and ministries have made this present construction possible; with prayer in faith for those who shall worship and minister in this place in days to come,

PEOPLE: We dedicate this house of God.

PASTOR: We now, as members of the household of God, in unity of spirit, in the love of Christ and in gratitude for this house to be an habitation of God through the Spirit,

PASTOR AND PEOPLE: We now dedicate ourselves to Christ, to the worship of God, to the work to which He has appointed us; now and for ever. Amen.

DECLARATION OF DEDICATION

The minister, or a denominational official, shall say:

In the name of the Father, and of the Son, and of the Holy Spirit, I now declare this house to be set apart forever from profane and common uses; and that it shall be set apart for worship and service of almighty God to whom belong "power, and riches, and wisdom, and strength, and honor, and glory, and blessing." Amen.

PRAYER

If the previous prayer was an invocation, this prayer should be for God's acceptance of the dedication. This prayer may also be one of consecration of the people. And it may be a benediction.

—William E. Pickthorn

A WEEK OF DEDICATION

SUNDAY MORNING—DEDICATION TO WORSHIP

ORGAN PRELUDE

CHOIR PROCESSIONAL

The song "Holy, Holy, Holy" is suggested.

INVOCATION

HYMN

The song "Come Thou Almighty King" is suggested.

RESPONSIVE READING

PASTOR: "How amiable are thy tabernacles, O Lord of hosts!

PEOPLE: My soul longeth, yea, even fainteth for the courts of the Lord: my heart and my flesh crieth out for the living God.

PASTOR: Yea, the sparrow hath found an house, and the swallow a nest for herself, where she may lay her young, even thine altars, O Lord of hosts, my King, and my God.

PEOPLE: Blessed are they that dwell in thy house: they will be still praising thee.

PASTOR: Blessed is the man whose strength is in thee; in whose heart are the ways of them.

PEOPLE: Who passing through the valley of Baca make it a well; the rain also filleth the pools.

119

PASTOR: They go from strength to strength, every one of them in Zion appeareth before God.

PEOPLE: O Lord God of hosts, hear my prayer: give ear, O God of Jacob.

PASTOR: Behold, O God our shield, and look upon the face of thine anointed.

PEOPLE: For a day in thy courts is better than a thousand. I had rather be a doorkeeper in the house of my God, than to dwell in the tents of wickedness.

PASTOR: For the Lord God is a sun and shield; the Lord will give grace and glory; no good thing will he withhold from them that walk uprightly.

PEOPLE: O Lord of hosts, blessed is the man that trusteth in thee."   (Ps. 84)

VOCAL SOLO

OFFERING

DEDICATION PRAYER

DEDICATION MESSAGE

BENEDICTION

SUNDAY AFTERNOON—DEDICATION TO PRAYER

ORGAN MEDITATION

CHOIR

"Spirit of the Living God" is suggested as a good prayer song.

SOLO

"Prayer Changes Things" is a suitable song.

DEDICATION PRAYER

DEDICATORIAL MESSAGE
CALL TO PRAYER

The congregation is divided so that some of the people go to each of the new rooms to dedicate it to service as they kneel in prayer.

SUNDAY NIGHT—DEDICATION TO EVANGELISM

ORGAN MELODIES
EVANGELISTIC SONG SERVICE
PRAYER
QUARTET
INSTRUMENTAL SOLO
CHOIR
OFFERING
VOCAL SOLO
DEDICATION PRAYER
DEDICATORIAL MESSAGE
BENEDICTION

MONDAY NIGHT—DEDICATION TO MUSIC

ORGAN SELECTIONS
SONGFEST
DEDICATION PRAYER
MUSICAL SELECTIONS

The choir and other vocal and instrumental groups may here present a concert of sacred music.

OFFERTORY AND OFFERING
DEDICATORIAL MESSAGE
BENEDICTION

121

TUESDAY NIGHT—DEDICATION TO CHURCH FELLOWSHIP

ORGAN MELODIES
SONG SERVICE
PRAYER
CHOIR
INTRODUCTIONS

Denominational officers, visiting ministers from other denominations, president of the local ministerial association, pastors of nearby churches, etc.

MUSICAL NUMBERS
OFFERING
DEDICATION PRAYER
DEDICATORIAL MESSAGE
BENEDICTION

WEDNESDAY NIGHT—DEDICATION TO CIVIC SERVICE

ORGAN PRELUDE
MALE CHORUS
SONG SERVICE
GREETINGS AND PRAYER

By a visiting civic official.

TRUMPET SOLO
QUARTET
INTRODUCTIONS

Visiting civic, club, and business officials.

OFFERING
QUARTET
DEDICATION PRAYER

DEDICATORIAL MESSAGE

BENEDICTION

THURSDAY NIGHT—DEDICATION TO MISSIONS

ORGAN MELODIES

SONG SERVICE

PRAYER

By a missionary guest.

HARP SOLO

VOCAL SOLO

INTRODUCTIONS

Visiting missionaries, missionaries supported by the church who are home on furlough.

CHOIR

DEDICATION PRAYER

OFFERING

VOCAL SOLO

DEDICATORIAL MESSAGE

To be delivered by a veteran missionary.

BENEDICTION

FRIDAY NIGHT—DEDICATION TO YOUTH

BAND CONCERT

Musical selections from a visiting band.

YOUTH CHORAL GROUP

Vocal and instrumental selections from the youth department of the church.

OFFERTORY AND OFFERING
Offertory played by the visiting band.
SOLO
DEDICATION PRAYER
DEDICATORIAL MESSAGE
BENEDICTION

SUNDAY MORNING—DEDICATION TO COMMUNION

HYMN
"Break Thou the Bread of Life" is suggested as suitable.
RESPONSIVE READING
First Corinthians 11:23-32, or some other selection from the section of this manual on The Lord's Supper may be used.
DEDICATION PRAYER
CHOIR
"Hallelujah, What a Saviour."
PRESENTATION OF NEW MEMBERS
OFFERING
VOCAL SOLO
DEDICATORIAL MESSAGE
HOLY COMMUNION
BENEDICTION

SUNDAY NIGHT—DEDICATION TO STEWARDSHIP

ORGAN PRELUDE

SONG SERVICE
PRAYER
MUSICAL PROGRAM
Unannounced selections by a quartet.
OFFERING
CHOIR
DEDICATION PRAYER
DEDICATORIAL MESSAGE
BENEDICTION
—Claire E. Britton